Philosophy for Passengers

Philosophy
for Passengers

Michael Marder

artwork by Tomás Saraceno

The MIT Press
Cambridge, Massachusetts
London, England

The MIT Press would like to thank the anonymous peer reviewers who provided comments on drafts of this book. The generous work of academic experts is essential for establishing the authority and quality of our publications. We acknowledge with gratitude the contributions of these otherwise uncredited readers.

This book was set in Arnhem Pro by Jen Jackowitz. Printed and bound in the United States of America.

Library of Congress Cataloging-in-Publication Data

Names: Marder, Michael, 1980- author. | Saraceno, Tomás,
   1973– illustrator.
Title: Philosophy for passengers / Michael Marder ; artwork by
   Tomás Saraceno.
Description: Cambridge, Massachusetts : The MIT Press, [2022] |
   Includes bibliographical references.
Identifiers: LCCN 2021031219 | ISBN 9780262543712 (paperback)
Subjects: LCSH: Air travel—Philosophy. | Air travel—Social aspects. |
   Aeronautics, Commercial—Passenger traffic—Social aspects.
Classification: LCC HE9787 .M373 2022 | DDC 387.7/42—dc23
LC record available at https://lccn.loc.gov/2021031219

10 9 8 7 6 5 4 3 2 1

publication supported by a grant from
The Community Foundation for Greater New Haven
as part of the **Urban Haven Project**

For my mother, the perennial passenger

Contents

Contents

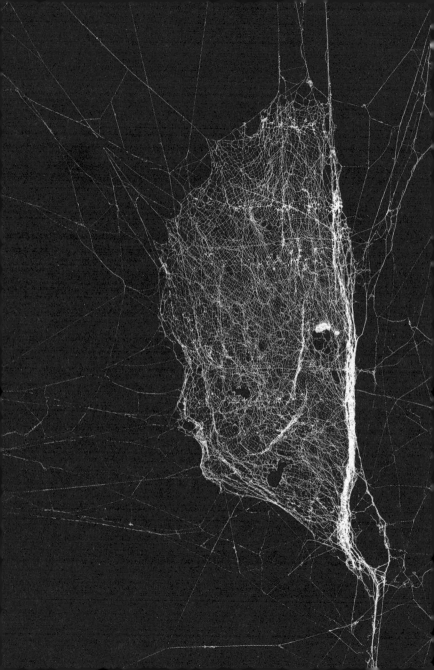

Ticketing

Judging by the extensive sections dedicated to it in bookstores, by the array of available magazines and myriads of blogs, travel is a topic in high demand. We have a nearly unquenchable thirst for travel: every destination seduces and whispers in our ears the names of others, yet unvisited and more exotic still. We feel that our lives will be incomplete unless we take a selfie in that picture-perfect spot and, after posting it on our social media accounts and putting a fresh check mark in our bucket list, move on to another line in the list, another place, a new adventure. Philosophers have caught wind of this facet of human desire. Alain de Botton's *The Art of Travel*, Daniel Klein's *Travels with Epicurus*, and Emily Thomas's *The Meaning of Travel* are just some recent titles in the budding field of "philosophy of travel."[1]

By comparison, written materials on passengers have been limited to dry technical safety manuals, sets of rules, or rights-and-obligations guidelines. Becoming a passenger is, at best, the boring bit we must do in order to travel to an exciting location beckoning us from the glossy pages of magazines and sleek entries in blogs. But what if we had at our disposal a sort of philosophical passenger handbook? Are we not frequently also passengers before, while, and after we are travelers? Does the meaning of travel not presuppose the meaning of being a passenger, or, in a word, *passengerhood*?

The dearth of reflections on passengerhood is a poor excuse for keeping it sidelined with a brief riposte that the matter is too trivial for the lofty activity of thinking. Assuming that the job of philosophy is to conduct an "inquiry into being as such and as a whole,"[2] every aspect of being is fit for its questioning impulse. More than that, every morsel of *what is*, no matter how insignificant it first appears, shines with the meaning of "being as such and as a whole." Being a passenger is no exception. We should not treat our activities and passivities as passengers tersely and dismissively, or, as the French might say, *en passant*.

Are we not frequently also passengers before, while, and after we are travelers?

Philosophy happens today neither in pondering the immutable realities of substance and divinity nor in scrutinizing the metaphysical nature of the subject and the will.[3] It happens in dwelling on the fleeting, the transient and the transitory, the ephemeral that survives what only yesterday appeared unshakeable. For instance, on dust.[4] Or on passengers.

What follows is not an allegory, not an intricate symbolic representation of deeper underlying issues through a specific, if a little extravagant in its commonality, extended example. Such an approach would transform the flesh-and-blood figures of passengers (that is, you and me) into philosophical figureheads. So, how can we avoid playing a symbolic game here? In at least two ways. (1) We will look into the minutiae of passenger experience, with a welter of its emotional and practical, temporal and spatial, social and economic attributes. (2) We will analyze this experience as the condensation and the distillation of our experience "as such and as a whole." A red thread running through our philosophical probing of the everyday will be the hunch that, in the twenty-first century, the experience of passengers is experience itself, well beyond the sphere of public and semipublic means of transport.

That is what I have signed up for in writing this book and what you are signing up for in starting to read it. That is our ticket for the upcoming trip.

Preboarding

An axiom of our mental optics: things come into sharper focus once we take a step back and stand at a distance from them. This axiom holds true for the experience of being a passenger, as well.

Whatever your reason for riding in a horse-drawn carriage, an auto rickshaw, or a bullock cart; for taking a bus or a streetcar, a taxi, or an Uber; for boarding a train, a plane, or a boat—using these and other means of transport makes you a passenger. To the minds of billions around the world, the experience is too routine to notice. Barely an issue, it borders on a nonexperience, something we live through without so much as taking cognizance of it, going through the motions unconsciously, on autopilot.

All this swiftly changed in the aftermath of the COVID-19 pandemic. With multiple restrictions, lockdowns, and quarantines, human mobility was undercut virtually overnight. Travel ground to a halt, was reduced, or dramatically restyled. Some passengers faced countless difficulties and impossibilities of passage—at the extreme, the quite unremarkable passage that crossing the threshold of the room, the apartment, or the house where one lives entails. Others, without the luxury of telework, had no choice but to board overcrowded public means of transport, apprehensive that their passengerhood could make them sick, putting their lives at risk.

That said, a drastic and unexpected reduction of human mobility during the pandemic had profound effects. (A hint: these had nothing to do with the temporary improvements in air and water quality as a result of decreases in the volumes of transport and industrial activities.) Staying put, remaining in place without the chance to move elsewhere, simply abiding, albeit nervously and impatiently, gave us a different perspective not only on travel but also on the passages that make up our day-to-day life, on the temporarily inaccessible experience of being a passenger, and on ourselves. And, in tandem with the *practical* problems that have suddenly cropped up, passengerhood flashed, at least in my mind, as a *theoretical* concern.

Beyond worries with and hindrances to human mobility, a hiatus in our passenger activities involves an overhaul that is more world-shattering than the temporary inability to take subway to work or fly to the Caribbean for a vacation would lead us to believe. In the instant when we are abruptly denied the possibilities we have tended to take for granted, a hidden infrastructure of our thinking and existence is revealed, somewhat like the seabed exposed by a receding tide. It turns out, then, that what I am calling passengerhood is an organizing principle behind our sense of time and space, not to mention our sense of sense, the paradigm of meaning in perpetual motion and of rapidly shifting sensory fields. I invite you to explore this existential seabed together with me, to take your seat, catch a ride, and become a passenger in this book on the philosophy of (and for) passengers.

The best time for reading a philosophical passenger handbook is the opposite of the time that is suitable for writing one. Insights into a phenomenon crystallize soon after our immersion in the matters at

Passengerhood is an organizing principle behind our sense of time and space, not to mention our sense of sense, the paradigm of meaning in perpetual motion and of rapidly shifting sensory fields.

hand has been seriously disrupted. But these same insights lend themselves to understanding in the midst of the very experience they seek to comprehend, redoubled with self-reflection. So, I wrote this text in a period of reduced global mobility, and I recommend reading it once the "simple" acts of catching a bus, a train, a boat, or a plane have resumed.

At any rate, if you are whiling your time on a trip—slightly bored and vaguely aware that there isn't more to time than this *meanwhile*—then the book you have just cracked open is for you. Especially, since, viewed under a philosophical microscope, the stretch of the *meanwhile* encompasses the time of a life.

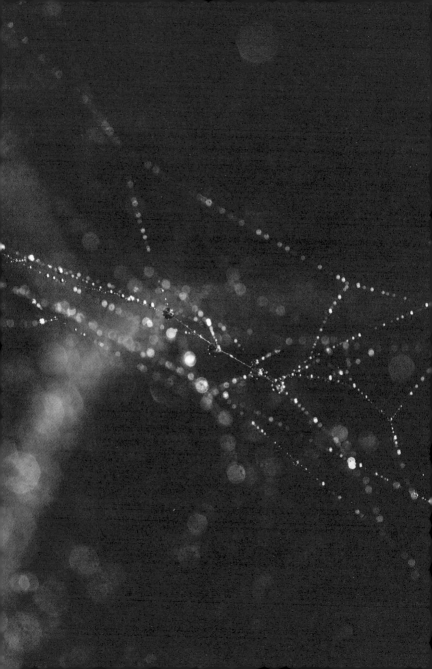

The Boarding Process (A): The Basics

To begin, consider the defining features of the role tacitly allotted to passengers in any mode and means of transport. Curiously enough, the portrait of passengerhood exhibiting these features will be riddled with glaring inconsistencies (indeed, with inner contradictions) as it embraces on an equal footing togetherness and loneliness, randomness and a strict socioeconomic order, activity and passivity. I claim that these contradictions are, far from vexing discrepancies, essential to the passenger position.

1. *Togetherness*. You cannot be a passenger without sharing a means of transport with others. Sharing runs the gamut from carpooling to sitting next to or behind a driver or the captain who steers a privately hired vehicle or vessel that carries you both. Such

togetherness means that your paths momentarily cross: you find yourselves in the same (mobile) place and time of a journey. What you and your fellow passengers have in common are the origin and the destination, which is also nowhere near certain, given that you might be in transit, making a connection there where the trips of others end. A driver or a captain shares time and space with you by dint of servicing that route. If animals (horses, donkeys, camels, oxen, dogs . . .) are involved, they are together with you for the duration of the journey. To be sure, though officially indifferent to the actual means of transport, the label *passenger* stubbornly sticks to someone riding in a mechanical conveyance. It is a modern term par excellence, the term that, coined in the fourteenth century and endowed with its current meaning in the sixteenth,[1] gains currency in modernity, when horse carriages give way to automobiles. That is why it silently and unjustifiably excludes animals, who nevertheless feel the proximity of the coachman or coachwoman on their skin and sense passengers as the sheer weight they pull. And why stop at animals? Might we not experience anonymous togetherness with the means of transport—a car, a boat, a plane? Once again, the people steering these machines are apt to feel more unity with them than the passengers they carry. Still, at some level, passengers know that their fates are bound up with that of the conveyance: they arrive in one piece together and fall to pieces also together.

2. *Loneliness.* Passenger togetherness goes hand in hand with the impression that you are alone in a crowd of travelers. A teenager who is listening to loud music in a subway car, drum-and-bass spilling over from their headphones; a businesswoman working away on her laptop during a transatlantic flight; a man agitatedly talking on his cellphone for the duration of an intercity bus ride; a person reading a book on a train . . . These are separate bubbles, worlds that barely intersect, except as bodies occupying a limited (often uncomfortably so) space for a stretch of time. Their worlds contract to the beats and rhythms displacing all else from the mental sphere; to an upcoming business meeting; to an all-consuming love quarrel; to a gripping plot of a novel. Occasional points of intersection among passengers are likely to provoke

frictions and irritation there where the bubble of the other (the bubble that *is* the other passenger) fails to match its ideally self-contained outlines. We are annoyed when the spheres of others expand, so that we are unwillingly drawn into their private worlds manifesting themselves at the visual, audible, tactile, or olfactory registers. The golden rule of reciprocity dictates that each must watch and police the boundaries of their own bubble to ensure peaceful coexistence for the time of the trip. Should all the passengers start talking loudly on their cellphones or listening to music at maximum volume, intolerable cacophony would ensue, preventing everyone from hearing and saying anything. "Silent cars" resolve such conflicts in advance, disallowing them in principle. They are, nonetheless, unable to do away with the mutual estrangement of individual bubbles, or what philosophers dub *alienation*, which they only exacerbate. The situation is hardly unique to public transportation. It is merely brought into sharper relief in that confined medium.

3. *Excess*. There are more passengers around us than we realize. I do not mean persons who hitch

a ride without buying a ticket, as in the reckless practice of "train surfing" or in the desperate attempts of stowaways to fly hidden in a plane's wheel well. In the seventeenth century, philosopher Gottfried Wilhelm Leibniz imagined matter as a garden within a garden within a garden . . . Pushing his materialism to a limit, we might say that there are imperceptible passengers who travel on human passengers, including microscopic creatures, such as bacteria and viruses. The incredibly quick global spread of COVID-19 is attributable to the nonhuman passenger excess that planes and cruise ships helped move around the world. Regardless of screening protocols and border controls, regardless of preboarding tests and health or vaccine certificates, this excess is ineliminable. We will always carry and let pass more passengers than we think are traveling aboard. Both on us and in us: in our breaths and saliva, on our clothes and hands, in our thoughts, fantasies, and dreams that, as secret pieces of luggage, we all carry. Wherever we pass, whomever we pass by, we will pass these things along, through projection and infection. We will smuggle them across borders and barriers, unbeknownst to the authorities and to ourselves. And no passport, health or otherwise, will change this situation.

4. *Passivity*. To be a passenger is to be transported by something and someone else, even as you, yourself, are the means of transport for indiscernible excess, both real and symbolic. It is to cede the active role of driving, guiding, steering, piloting, navigating, or conducting to the other (person or machine, as in the case of inertial navigation systems). As a passenger, you are not in a position to do anything to facilitate the trip, apart from refraining from causing a commotion. There is undeniably something passive and receptive in the role of the passenger, in which passivity is tied into a conceptual knot with passing, with the past, and with passion in the original sense of *pathos*, an undergoing at the foundations of all experience. Like passivity with respect to cooking at a restaurant where one dines, passenger passivity comes with a price tag. We pay for others to fetch, process, and prepare food for us, just as we pay for others to transport us. But, unlike a diner's receptivity in a restaurant, the passivity of a passenger functions on a different timescale

of enjoyment: a meal is consumed *after* a chef has prepared and a waiter or a courier has delivered it, whereas a trip is taken *simultaneously* with drivers, pilots, and crew members guiding and servicing the route of a plane or a train, with which they are partly identified in the passenger's mind. Passive and active roles overlap in the time and space of a trip, in which the passive position is advantageous. This begs the questions: traveling all alone by car, are you your own chauffeur and passenger, the driving and the driven, in the latest incarnation of the philosophical subject-object relation? How do driverless cars change the dynamics of passenger-hood and the allocation of subject and object positions? What is the fate of activity when passivity waxes absolute?

5.   *Activity*. The mental flower that blooms most vigorously on the branches of passenger passivity is boredom. To confess, I often find myself in this state during my travels. Boredom is not inherently bad or reprehensible. You peer out of a train window, failing to notice the landscape you quickly leave behind. Or you stare at a computer game on your phone and dexterously press buttons,

reclining in your plane seat. You may look at the floor of the subway car you are in or at your hands or shoes, painstakingly avoiding crossing glances with fellow passengers. What else is there to do when the work of moving from place to place is performed by someone or something else—a horse, a tram, a captain? And that is precisely the point: the opportunity to be carried along without exerting any effort *frees* you for many other pursuits. Boredom is a symptom of subjection to this body and mind that you are in the here-and-now that seems to last forever. But it is also a harbinger of freedom, concentrated, at minimum, in an unstated decision to keep an array of activities in the shape of untapped possibilities. It could be that, bored of being bored, you begin to think (ruminate, muse, free-associate) and do something (not necessarily productive), embracing an activity reinvigorated by the ennui that had preceded it. Whether or not boredom looms large on psychic horizons, the field for passenger activity is opened up and kept open by the passivity of being transported, coupled with the impression of having a space and a time apart from the physical locales of home and work, of school and a vacation spot, of a conference venue and a retreat. The impression of being in-between. Unoccupied by tasks that would fill them, the space and the time of passengerhood are, hence, *occupiable* by a whole range of things . . . or by nothing in particular.

6. *Randomness*. If day in, day out, you board the same bus at the same hour from the same stop, odds are you'll start meeting a core group of passengers, who commute on the same route. This is a highly predictable set of circumstances. But, generally, the following rule applies: the less local your passenger experience, the more random the group of people who happen to share a means of transport with you. In densely populated metropolitan areas, on planes and trains, passengers are comparable to billiard balls sent by an intangible cue stick along an identical trajectory. (Since John Locke and David Hume, philosophers adore the billiard analogy.) Unless you travel with friends, family, fellow students, or coworkers, the people sitting next to you are there by fluke, even if their stated preference was an aisle or a window seat. After the fashion of anonymous mass societies, where such

travel flourishes, it is difficult to experience genuine togetherness in chance convergence of social atoms. With the exception of carpooling, commuters do not form a community; neither do other kinds of passengers.

7. *Classed order*. The randomness of passenger convergences masks a rigidly stratified order they are part of. Business, economy, executive, first, second, premium, standard: these are just some of the class designations for passengers who are prompted to replicate the dynamics of the socioeconomic classes they belong to during their travels. Buses and trams are, of course, more egalitarian, provided that their front and back sections are not segregated by race or gender. (In countries such as Mexico and China, depending on the amenities they offer, buses are subdivided into luxury, plus, first, and second categories.) In many instances, however, these are the means of transport used by people who do not own a car. Physical distances and proximities between passengers are expressions of the proximities and distances between them as members of their respective classes. The intangible cue stick mutates, all of a sudden, into the invisible hand of the market.

The Boarding Process (A)

With the exception of carpooling, commuters do not form a community; neither do other kinds of passengers.

The Boarding Process (B): The Passenger Society

There is no community of passengers, but we live in a passenger society. From the Latin *societas*, a society is an association, more an accompaniment than a company of those who follow (*sequi*), those who come after and go second (*secundus*). Twitter, with its millions of followers, expresses the truth of society in the digital age. Passengers personify this truth as it applies to physical mobility. Each group of passengers thrown together by a mix of chance and class is a transitory society of transients. And so, also, is the larger society we live in, which is encapsulated in the microcosm of passenger realities.

Take, for instance, the tense combination of togetherness and loneliness in passenger experience. Is that not a nifty way to describe our contemporary societies? The numbers of single people living in big cities are rising steadily; in the United States, they account for more than 45 percent of the population.[1] Living alone among millions of others, many of them probably also single, is like riding a bus without a stop, at which you might get off. More than a particular historical interpretation of the social, ours is society at its purest: society as opposed to community, *Gesellschaft* rather than *Gemeinschaft*, in a distinction emphasized by sociologist Ferdinand Tönnies. It is a togetherness based on impersonal contracts and formal roles (as in passengerhood) instead of blood, family, and clan, among other natural, personal, direct ties and their attendant value systems. No wonder, then, that the root of the word *society* is responsible for the formation of both *association* and *sequestering*!

Loneliness in the midst of multitudes triggers depression and anxiety, feeding a growing pharmaceutical industry. On its desolate terrain, one cannot act. Further, in a state of loneliness, one is nothing but one: neither you nor I nor we . . . Each passenger and each member of our societies is, by default, such a one, which does not mean that all of us must remain in that state.

Having fled the horrors of Nazi Germany, philosopher Hannah Arendt warns that loneliness foments the rise of totalitarian regimes: "What prepares men for totalitarian domination in the non-totalitarian world is the fact that loneliness, once a borderline experience suffered in certain marginal social conditions like old age, has become an everyday experience of the ever-growing masses of our century."[2] To extend Arendt's line of reasoning, we might conjecture that passenger experience is proto-totalitarian. Passivity leads directly to loneliness, the loneliness saturating the universe of "totalitarian domination" and that enveloping passenger pastimes. But Arendt does not advocate minimizing the opportunities of being alone; more nuanced, she praises "the productive potentialities of isolation" and wishes to increase the "chances that loneliness may be transformed into solitude."[3] Do passengers not transition from passivity to activity, because and to the extent that their loneliness has been transformed into solitude? If so, then what does solitude actually mean?

In solitude, one begins to imagine oneself in the shape of an I. You find yourself face-to-face with yourself, not alone among countless others, but *alone with yourself* in the rarefied air of boredom. A different kind of sequestering and another sort of association are necessary for the elementary unit of sociality (I-myself) to emerge. This unit supplants the passenger bubbles and the equally spherical billiard balls we have spotted earlier. As a relation, as a fecund failure of the I to coincide with myself, "I" count as not-one and, therefore, as both more and less than one. I am, at once, the first and the second with regard to myself; I predate and follow myself in a strange variation on the *sequi* of *societas*. Essentially over and above myself in myself, it is starting from solitude that I can forge genuine relations with others and unleash my creativity, which may be understood as an overflow of my self-relation, not an arcane effect of "inspiration" or "genius."

In our passenger societies filled to the brim with loneliness, solitude is a rare beast. Some of the culprits to be blamed for its infrequency are the social media that are, indeed, social, in that they are the tools of associating and sequestering, sequestering *in* associating, their users. The ideal connectivity they promote is antithetical to physical, spatial interconnectedness. That is why you are closer to a person who is hundreds of kilometers away and with whom you are in a chatroom or a messaging app at the moment than to the passenger in the seat next to yours. Gradually, or not so gradually, family and friends appear in the same dim and sterile light as that passenger: although seated around the dinner table, each is in a separate bubble of proximity to online contacts and distance from those with whom the meal is shared.

The tragedy of ideal connectivity is the absence of holes in the web of total communication. One is sequestered, imprisoned in oneself by constant, infinitely ramified association. Concocted from inexhaustible possibilities of staying in touch, freedom is a heavy burden, since only a tiny fraction of these possibilities may be put into practice, leaving us chronically unfulfilled. It devours our time and, therefore, it devours *us*, seeing that time is the cloth from which we are all cut. Physical transit may provide a much-needed break from ideal connectivity, the passengers' separation from their points of departure and destinations amplified by their being offline. (This condition is, lamentably, becoming a thing of the past aboard planes, to say nothing of trains and buses, boasting their own Wi-Fi systems.) I do some of my best writing when, as a passenger, I am disconnected from the internet, away from email, the newsfeed, and the like. I can still match in my mind sundry passages in my books and articles to particular airports and flights, train stations and journeys, bus and subway rides, when and where they were first written.

Despite its segregationist overtones, the division of passenger zones into classes reinforces the societal dimension of passengerhood. "Second class" is what makes the passenger arrangement social. In numerical order, it admittedly follows the first, but "first class" is only first because there is the second coming after it. Similarly, if less counterintuitively, there is no "business" without "economy." The existence of second class makes first class what it is: more comfortable, more expensive, more prestigious compared to other classes. Were there to be a single class accommodating all, we would have a classless passenger experience of everyone traveling with an equal degree of comfort, legroom, service, and number of bathrooms per person. That, in miniature, is a variation on the Marxist theme of *klassenlose Gesellschaft*, a classless society, in which the difference between the first and the second, as much as between the first and the last, has been abolished. A society-less society, perhaps?

In case you need additional proof of the mirroring that goes on between passenger classes and their socioeconomic equivalents, observe the process of their (ideological) complexification. The disparities between the rich and the poor are widening on a worldwide scale, a tendency that is consistent with Marx's expectation of ongoing class polarization. And, just the reverse, socially coded class distinctions are continually refined: the middle class is further subdivided into the upper and the lower, while, in the US context, the five classes as determined by Gallup are upper, upper-middle, middle, working, and lower.[4] Does this complexification not correspond to the intermediate classes in air travel, slotted between first and economy: business, premium economy, and economy plus? The social hierarchy grows more robust, the more the ideological apparatus that goes with it instills a conviction in my mind that there is someone second to me, and a third to that second, all the way down the ladder. The travel industry, which is a misnomer for the passenger industry, is invested in safeguarding and perpetuating the illusions of class mobility that go along with this conviction: economy passengers believe that second to *them* are those who cannot afford flying at all.

The travel industry, which is a misnomer for the passenger industry, is invested in safeguarding and perpetuating the illusions of class mobility.

In this respect, it is important to remember that there is an infrastructural mesh of people and technologies that do not leave their places and that, in not moving, facilitate the mobility of others. I am thinking of janitorial staff at train stations, of workers and machines handling baggage at airports, of track maintenance people and equipment in subway tunnels . . . Theirs is the largely inconspicuous (and, in the case of humans, underpaid) labor of producing passengers as passengers, of rendering passenger flows efficient and unobstructed. Plenty of energy needs to be expended on the ground for passenger society to get off the ground and to function. The aggregate of this energy forms the outer limit of passengerhood, participating in passenger dynamics by way of being excluded from them.

The inflexible demarcation lines, carving up passenger society, fail to eliminate the excess that disrespects every conceivable system or grid. The wild, untamable excess has to do with passages, with passing in and out, with passing through. Border closures in response to the COVID-19 pandemic intended to do away not so much with virus importation from abroad (in retrospect, the countries that closed themselves

Stop no. 1: Mood

You may be in a mood to travel if you feel like exploring territories and waters that, for you, are still uncharted, or if you just wish to relax on a beach, visit city monuments, or backpack in the mountains or in the countryside. Is there a comparable passenger mood, independent of the goal that impels you to ride a train or a bus, to sail on a boat or to catch a taxi? How can we deduce such a mood from the mental hues of our experiences?

Boredom

Passengers are the throngs of people (not only the human kind[1]) who pass through what stays in place and apparently does not pass: airports and train stations, fields and forests, boulevards and alleys, the waves licking the stern of a cruise ship or the mountain ranges beneath the wings of an airplane. This stability, too, is an illusion: the places we pass through are altered at whirlwind pace owing to, among other things, the dynamics of climate change. Actually, our passing through them *en masse* contributes a great deal to their alteration by way of noise pollution and CO_2 emissions. We draw the entire world into the vortex of passengerhood.

The changing scenery on the other side of the window fizzles out into a relatively uniform haze. As passengers, we leave behind what we pass either too quickly for details to be discernible or too slowly to pique our interest and awaken our overstimulated senses. The landscape is incredibly far from us when we fly ten thousand meters above it or when we delve deep underneath it in the subway system; it is occluded by the backs of other passengers on a crowded bus, or distant from the world of our private concerns while we stare at our changing surroundings without noticing them. Nondifferentiation breeds indifference, a disengaged neutral mood conducive to boredom.

Bored with outside reality, you might want to turn inward, swathing yourself in your daydreams and thought fragments, desires and regrets, reminiscences and aspirations. You may nap to the even noise of the engines and pace of movement. Should you do so, you would be traveling *in yourself* without budging from your seat: you would be orbiting yourself, exploring the nooks and crannies of your inner universe, while moving arrowlike through space. At the same time, nothing prevents you from getting as bored with the inside as with the outside, aloof to your psychic and physical passengerhood. We've seen, in passing, how boredom can revive activity and creativity. But what if this mood has staying power? What if it lingers on?

Persistent boredom is an extremely prevalent disposition in our day and age. An affective hallmark of the times, it frequently permeates the passenger experience. For German philosopher Martin Heidegger, this "pallid, evenly balanced lack of mood, which is often persistent and which is not to be mistaken for a bad mood, is far from nothing at all. Rather, it is in this that existence becomes satiated with itself. Being has become manifest as a burden."[2]

Boredom plays a vital role in unveiling who we are: finite creatures subjected to time in thought and in deed. The manifest burden of being is that of time elapsing in an excruciatingly slow manner, with nowhere else to go and nothing to occupy it (or us), despite the entertainment at our disposal or the work at our fingertips. The emptiness of this time that is only mine is its absolute fullness, its satiation with itself, my satiation with myself. I see my life with utmost clarity in this medium, unobstructed by things to do, to acquire, or to brag about. Bored passengers become the passages for empty time, the time of a voyage, in the course of which they encounter only themselves with nowhere to hide, again, from themselves.

Anxiety

The experience of boredom is certainly jarring, provided that no activity is capable of lifting us out of it. But it is only one strand of our vulnerability. To be a passenger is to be susceptible to a number of fears and phobias, from the claustrophobia-inducing crammed means of transportation and tunnels to the agoraphobia-provoking crowded airports or bus and train stations, from the fear of flying to that of getting sick abroad, or the more general hodophobia, the fear of travel.[3] The dread and anxiety forming the comet tail of boredom have little in common with these phobias. That is because anxiety and dread are sparked off by something other than a definite fear-inducing object, be it a plane, a tunnel, a crowd, an illness, or what have you. Their vagueness, diffuse nature, and unattached character are clues to the traits of the thing that acts as their cause.

The absence of a recognizable source makes the negative sentiments that extend their tentacles out of boredom exceptionally difficult to cope with. When all is said and done, there is no identifiable enemy behind them, no debilitating stimulus that would be open to a gradual psychological reconditioning. The quiet angst of solitary existence in the "pallid" state of boredom indicates our trepidation in the face of finitude, a fear of death, which also does not fit the mold of a discernible object with sharp outlines and profiles. While it is true that, in terms of their psychological dynamics, phobias have little in common with the moods and emotions boredom generates, they might be rooted in the same overarching and free-floating affect as the one our undying, if for the most part backgrounded, awareness of mortality enkindles. And, since passengers find themselves on their way, in transit—which may never be completed as intended, all statistical assurances about the infrequency of accidents notwithstanding—their mood overlays the physical passage they are making in their travels with the possibility of passing away, a euphemism for death.

French philosopher Jacques Derrida confides in a letter dated May 10, 1997, to his former student and colleague Catherine Malabou: "I never go away on a trip, I don't *go*, I never put any distance whatsoever between me and my 'house' without thinking—with images, films, drama, and full orchestral soundtrack—that I am going to die before I return."[4] Any passenger experience may turn out to be a one-way ticket. But what is the difference between dying at home, "in my 'house,'" as Derrida writes, and on a trip? Are his lines symptomatic of a certain fear, the phobia of falling ill and dying abroad?

Things are a little knottier than a straightforward psychological interpretation would lead us to believe. What Derrida highlights is the unexpected including a mood that seems too insipid or too neutral to color any of our perceptions and experiences. In the passages in which passengers find themselves, moods are frequently determined by a time orientation that skirts the trip altogether, enthralled as passengers often are with what happened before and what might happen after it. Their minds inhabiting, by anticipation, the destination or dwelling, thanks to the workings of memory, at the point of departure, passengers gloss over the places they pass through. I am certain that, like me, you have often drawn the curtains or closed the window blinds next to your seat, pretending that there is nothing out there on the other side of the glass—that is to say, nothing worth your while.

In our heads, we live in the past or in the future, lagging behind or running ahead of ourselves, oblivious to the present, indifferent to a vanishing and instantly resurfacing stretch, the passage that we *are*. Perhaps, then, we've gotten everything wrong: it is not we, the passengers, who pass through immobile places; we remain mentally fixed, fixated on the future or on the past and physically stationary in a moving vessel or vehicle, whereas the world outside us moves, unfolding and contracting, changing, growing, decaying. How are we to keep pace with the dash of places and times, while taking care not to get mentally, if not bodily, seasick or motion sick?

Distraction is key. Rather than the denial of attention, it is the kind of hyperattention that frantically tries to live up to the maddening and ever accelerating speed of reality itself. In a distracted mood, we are mentally dispersed beyond the scatter of our gazes, leaping from thing to another poorly perceived thing at a blink of an eye. This quality makes it a promising cognitive candidate for the job of keeping pace with the physical displacement of people, if not of the places themselves. "Wait a moment!" you may object. "The movement you are talking about is not at all scattered: a train progresses toward its end goal—the last stop, the final destination—in a deliberate and sustained fashion, similar to an attentive regard concentrated on its target. What would distracted, dispersed, or scattered transport look like? Who would want to be a passenger on such a train?"

Lest we forget, not all passengers are traveling to the same destination, even when they are riding an express. Scatter applies to passenger experience, as well as to the nearly unlimited combinations of the limited and fixed aerial, terrestrial, or marine routes. In addition, what we are facing here is not a glitch in the goal-orientated nature of a movement, but its orientation to several goals in parallel. An exuberant striving of our curiosities and concerns in multiple directions, distraction replicates at the mental level the many trajectories of individual passengers or the exuberant growth of plant roots and branches. As the fracturing of attention, distraction strains to accompany the movement of the present in the present, in which each second splinters into n events.

With regard to a distracted appreciation of works of art, the essayist and cultural critic Walter Benjamin chose the model of architecture and, later on, the cinematic experience. "Distraction and concentration," he wrote, "form polar opposites which may be stated as follows: A man who concentrates before a work of art is absorbed by it. . . . In contrast, the distracted mass absorbs the work of art. This is most obvious with regard to buildings. Architecture has always represented the prototype of a work of art the reception of which is consummated by a collectivity in a state of distraction. The laws of its reception are most instructive."[5] Benjamin's "reception . . . in a state of distraction" dovetails may take its cues from the deracination of architecture. Our reception of mobile architecture in the state of distraction determines in advance our distracted mood as passengers. Needless to say, this is not the only mood reigning over passenger experience, but all the others must be imperceptibly won over from it, more so than from boredom, to occupy their place under the sun.

While you await boarding or rest in your passenger seat, your gaze travels, scanning the screen of your smartphone, glancing at fellow passengers, looking out the window. Your gaze may also be fixed on a single point, nearly unseeing, unreactive to the outside world, your thoughts racing, jumping from one impression to the next, bouncing from one sliver of memory to another. What or whom are you distracted from at any given moment? From your surroundings? From yourself? From the passage you make at present, the passage that is the present, or the passenger that you are?

Let's say you are distracted from yourself. You are then looking for an external diversion that would bury a mass of associations, desires, regrets, and ruminations under the seductive (as well as sedating, despite the excitement they generate) sights and sounds of entertainment. For a time being, the diversion will blunt your awareness of these mental torrents. But it will not eliminate them altogether. They will keep swirling under the thin coating of reception in a state of distraction (from yourself, above all) provided by inflight entertainment or by the movies you watch on your tablet while on a train.

Elation

The exhilaration of travel is understandable. You are on the verge of a discovery, of new contacts and connections with people and places you are unfamiliar with. What about the experience of being a passenger? Can it, in and of itself, be a source of elation and joy?

It stands to reason that the joy of passengerhood would be the lot of those who travel infrequently, those who have little or no opportunities to board the means of transport that elicit their excitement. The teenagers happily taking selfies at an airport or on a plane might not do the same at a bus station or on a bus. Beyond serving as the outward expressions of joy, these acts contribute to a snowballing digital archive, the sublime snapshot of the contemporary epoch. As they instantaneously migrate to the social media, travel and passenger selfies display elation intended for the consumption of other Facebook, Twitter, or Instagram users.

The staged joy of a passenger selfie is perceived as a token of genuine emotion, an authentic mood, both by the person who takes it and by those who will end up skimming over it in their feed. It must appear spontaneous, its staging hidden from everyone's view for the mood to be in effect. Gone is the traditional contrast between an actor's craft and a spur-of-the-moment emotion, between artifice and naturalness. The truth-index of joy, sadness, excitement, and boredom is their external appearance available for automatic judgments by the digital others and for codification in emojis. Selfies circle back to the self to forget it more thoroughly, amplifying the effects of distraction. This return to the self via a passenger selfie also freezes and neutralizes the passage—not only transience, but also transit and the possibility of a radical transition it holds.

If what we flee *from* is boredom, with its premonition of death, then what we flee *toward* is happiness, neatly framed in a selfie and symbolized by a smiley. Just listen to Nietzsche: "We who *flee* to happiness—:

we who need every kind of south and unruly fullness of sun and position ourselves at that point on the street where life, like a drunken parade of grotesque masks—like something that makes us lose our minds—tumbles past; we who demand of happiness *that* it makes us 'lose our minds': does it not seem that we have a knowledge that we *fear*?"[6]

"A drunken parade of grotesque masks" (selfies?) no longer tumbles past the passengers; instead, they (we) tumble along with it. Does this mean that, traveling for business or for pleasure, passengers finally live in these passages, considering that the parade is of life itself? Nietzsche thinks so: the inebriation of grotesque masks on a parade "makes us 'lose our minds,'" as though by contagion. *That* is happiness, elation, joy, toward which we flee. Unbeknownst to passengers, alcohol consumption during long trips may be motivated by a literal interpretation of this equation, as much as by the desire to muffle the insufferable rumble of the present-as-passage and, therefore, as fleeting, as no-longer-present in the present. To flee, in the same gesture, *from* and *toward*.

When crew members wish passengers a "pleasant journey," I hear a dash of cruel irony in their words.

How pleasant can the passenger experience be when you are crammed in your seat, with little fresh air, too hot or miserably cold, and sleep deprived? The excitement that comes along with novelty might compensate for all these discomforts to the point of ousting them from the sphere of consciousness. Those who are used to boarding fully booked or even overbooked flights, packed trains, or overcrowded buses might also overlook the negatives. For the rest of us, falling somewhere between these two categories, an appropriate wish should be: "Have a not-so-painful journey!"

Stop no. 2: Time

Under different guises and on various pretexts, we have been discussing nothing but time thus far, and we will surely keep revolving around this subject for the time to come. What are the parameters of time in the passenger experience?

We should, in the first place, sweep misunderstandings aside. "Passenger time" is not a reference to the duration of a trip, as measured by the clock: twenty minutes, two hours, eight and a half hours . . . Nor is it the time of departure or the hour of arrival at a destination, with the relevant questions of whether trains or buses, boats or planes, keep to the schedule and whether you are on time at the station, port, or terminal. What I am interested in is the passengers' *sense* of time, which may help disclose the sense of time *as such*.

While the clock synchronizes our activities and permits us, for instance, to board that 7:55 a.m. flight or 2:30 p.m. bus, each of us confronts the flux of time in a unique, idiosyncratic way. The experience of time depends largely on the mood you are in: bored, you feel time dragging on, a thick, viscous substance, in which you are bogged down; excited, you have an impression that time flies, almost too fast for you to obey the *carpe diem* injunction. As a branch of philosophy, phenomenology studies, among other things, multiple subjective perspectives on time, or, technically speaking, time-consciousness.

Whatever the speed at which it seems to flow, time passes. We pass with it and in it. There is a tinge of fatalism about that passage in Virgil's *Georgics*: "fugit inreparabile tempus," "irretrievably, time escapes" (III.284). So, time is to be sought in passing, in a passage, a stretch or a stretching that determines its activity as time. We are, all of us, time's passengers, witnesses to its passing, which is also our own. Time travel in science fiction follows on the heels of time's passage. As passengers on any means of transport, we are, therefore, reflecting time's activity. That is why passengerhood gives us a privileged perspective on this philosophical and existential leitmotif.

For millennia, human mobility has structured our thinking of time. Changes of place have been the signs and measures of time, ever since the Mesopotamian *Epic of Gilgamesh* and Homer's *Odyssey*. Even if its shape was circular—the narrative arc bent, the end meeting the beginning—an epic journey defined time-imagination all the way to the nineteenth century, with Hegel's *Phenomenology of Spirit* for its pinnacle.[1] The time of an epic relied on coherent plot development, where the final denouement both overshadowed and retrospectively shed light on the rest of the story. Gilgamesh's failure to attain immortality, Odysseus's return home to Ithaca, and Spirit's reunification with itself in absolute knowing bestowed the ultimate sense on all previous events in their respective stories and made other changes of place and time insubstantial by comparison.

As grand master narratives and traditionally authoritative sources of meaning came under attack in late modernity, and as travels started weaving the social fabric instead of puncturing it, the thinking of time underwent a number of momentous modifications.

Transition, transit, and transformation prevailed over the original, more or less static, state and the end result alike. The departure and the destination paled in significance compared to the middle. In keeping with Taoist philosophy and with the old German proverb "Der Weg ist das Ziel," the path became the goal.

Twentieth-century physics faithfully reflects this shift. Quantum mechanics elucidates the interference of the observer with the observed, the act of observation meddling with the reality it registers. In Einstein's general theory of relativity, gravity bends time (or, more accurately, the spacetime field around an object); in his special theory of relativity, time slows down or accelerates depending on how fast you travel in relation to something else. An emphasis on observation at the quantum level and on relation in relativity is the emphasis on that which is in-between two or more elements, in contrast to free-standing, independent, autonomous objects and subjects. By the same logic, the temporal crux of passengerhood is the perceived and measurable duration in a passage between places (and between times—especially, of departure and arrival) that is not subject to the purpose-driven, goal-oriented concerns of a journey, a trip, or traveling. It is as if, in the time of passengers, time came into its own precisely by refusing to come into its own, by refusing to be reconciled with a higher end that would extinguish its unrest.

To get into this temporal mindset, try examining your life from the perspective of transit and transition periods, instead of departures, arrivals, and phases of staying put. View the places you leave and those that welcome you from the middle of the passages stretching between them, not the other way around. The main events of our lives are also framed in the middle, between further events, their past and future horizons extending all the way to the objective framing of human life between birth and death. Intriguingly, these cardinal points of our existence are inaccessible to our consciousness as a pure beginning and end. The time of our lives passes between two black boxes, two Xs, two vanishing poles: unrepresentable, unreachable. Life is a middle passage without the shores to sail from or to moor at. In a paraphrase of the seventeenth-century French mathematician, theologian, and father of the first modern form of public transport[2] Blaise Pascal, who, in his turn, paraphrased fifteenth-century thinker Nicholas of Cusa, life is an infinitely finite sphere, of which the middle is everywhere and the circumference nowhere.

In the paradigm of the time that passes—the time that is marked principally by its activity of passing, the activity indistinguishable from the passivity of *pathos*—the past is the predominant tense. For passengers on a train, a bus, a plane, or any other means of transport, every place they leave behind immediately transitions from spatial into temporal terms: they move past it, and the instant of having cut through it drifts into the past. The future is cobbled together from portions of air, sea, or land routes not yet left behind but potentially convertible into the past, that is, prepared for passenger experience. Armed with a whole arsenal of recording technologies, we make memories for ourselves. The present stands no chance. Born old, it is on the verge of passing and, by the time it is presented (or re-presented) before our perception and cognition, it is no longer present.

Passengers, who pass with and as the time that passes, may be divided into two groups unrelated to the conventional classes. The first strive to *pass* the time (of a trip or of a life); the second endeavor to *make* time for sundry pursuits. I am taking note of this division without implying any positive or negative value judgment on either group, between which we all alternate depending on the circumstances. Those who wish just to pass the time may not be particularly productive or alert, as they take a nap onboard or resort to anything that would blunt their senses and stifle . . . what? The evidence of time as such, with which we are ceaselessly bombarded in our role as passengers. Passing the time within time's passage is letting oneself be carried along—not only by the means of transport one utilizes, but also by duration, by the seemingly unending stretch of a passage from A to B. Zeno's paradoxes nicely illustrate this glimmer of realization that we try to put out of our minds the moment it hits us, passengers, with all its disconcerting might.

According to the so-called dichotomy paradox, "however near is the mobile to any given point, it will always have to cover the half, and then the half of that, and so on without limit before it gets there" (Aristotle, *Physics* VI, 9, 239b). Suppose your bus is within 100 meters of a stop. It will first have to cover half that distance (i.e., 50 meters), and half of that half (i.e., 25 meters), and so on, before it reaches the stop, if ever. Infinity lurks within a finite period; each voyage takes an eternity. Duration is perdurance. If passing time as a passenger is tantamount to passing an eternity, a life sentence encrypted in every bus ride, then why not pass this time in total oblivion of its passage?

In another of Zeno's paradoxes, the super-fast runner Achilles can never overtake a tortoise. Why? Because "the slowest will never be overtaken in its course by the swiftest, inasmuch as, reckoning from any given instant, the pursuer, before he can catch the pursued, must reach the point from which the pursued started at that instant, and so the slower will always be some distance in advance of the swifter" (Aristotle, *Physics* VI, 9, 239b). Assuming that you travel in a horse-drawn carriage that departs from a station five minutes ahead of a high-speed train, the train will never catch up with the horse, because by the time it reaches a mark the horse will have already passed, the animal will have advanced a little more in relation to the mechanical means of transport, and again *ad infinitum*. For Zeno, a horse moves faster than a train from the vantage point of human thought that breaks the line of movement down into an infinity of points. Just passing the time of a journey is surrendering to the inevitable lag of our latest technologies vis-à-vis the speed and the demands of thought.

Passengers who want to do no more than pass a trip with the least awareness are reacting to the too-much of time weighing on them. Those who, in a caffeine-drenched state, struggle to make time for work or "active rest" are responding to the chronic not-enough of time. These two kinds of passengers belong together in a strange combination that slips infinity into finitude. In a dance of figure and ground, passing the time that apparently refuses to come to an end is foregrounding the infinite, whereas making time that ostensibly runs out before we have it at our disposal is concentrating on the finite. On the one hand, we pass the slowly elapsing, nearly still time; on the other, we experience time itself as ineluctably passing, the moment entirely swallowed up by the past before it has had a chance to make itself known. This is the temporal scheme of passengerhood, today's unmoved mover.

Detour no. 1: *¡No pasarán!*

A battle cry: "They shall not pass!" We are familiar with it from the Spanish Civil War, when Dolores Ibárruri Gómez uttered the famous words in her speech on the eve of the 1936 Battle for Madrid.[1] (After the victory of the Nationalist forces, Franco's response to the Communist slogan was "¡Ya hemos pasado!," "We have already passed!"[2]) But the words, denying passage to an enemy, have a longer history than we credit them with. In World War I, General Robert Nivelle appealed to the troops during the Battle of Verdun with the same slogan in French: "Ils ne passeront pas!" What do these words say to us, living over a hundred years later?

First of all, that, in an extreme situation of an armed conflict, there is no guaranteed passage without resistance, friction, and loss of life. More broadly, the slogan conveys that to pass is to pass *through* and that the ease or difficulty of passage depends on the degree of thickness and permeability of the medium through which one passes. The act of passing through is trespassing. "They shall not pass!" implies that *we*, who are locked in mortal combat against *them*, will make sure that they will not cross the lines separating us from them. At the extreme, we might be willing to turn our own bodies and lives into materials that will seal off the porous membranes between us, forging an impermeable wall out of our very existence. The enemies cannot be passengers in our world. In addition to denying them passage, we block their passengerhood, in all its temporal and spatial aspects, and, along with it, their belonging to a world. As a result, we cannot pass either; we deny ourselves the very thing of which we deprive the others. A political indigestion, a stoppage of systemic metabolism of sorts . . .

And doesn't the current situation of COVID-19 follow the same rule? Did the pandemic not disclose an analogous difficulty of passage, from border closures, through flight and train cancelations, to strict lockdowns? The world itself lost the veneer of transparency and permeability it had been endowed with in the eyes of the privileged few in the era of globalization. We no longer have the illusion of being able to pass through places without, each time anew, crossing the Rubicon. Political discourses of a "war on the virus" also made it appear that the slogan *¡No pasarán!* would apply to those already infected, regardless of the fact that new battle lines had to be drawn within and through the bodies of everyone without exception, given a high percentage of undetected asymptomatic infections. The difficulty of passage thus has to do not only with closed borders but also with fear and an awareness of the dangers inherent in being a passenger.

Our passengerhood became blocked along the physical and the metaphysical axes: a decrease in public transport ridership and a less perceptible alteration in what has come to be a fundamental condition of being in the world. For a short while, we could not be passengers, and that was enough to shake our passenger attitude toward reality to the core. Who can be a passenger without planes, trains, buses, ships, without passports, visas, or health certificates, and, more importantly, without a symbolic and material universe bolstering our passenger mentality? It is in this blockage, in this external resistance to and impossibility of passing (in a word, in this impassibility), that the truth of being a passenger began to emerge in the manner of a photographic negative—as much by virtue of the distance it opened between us and our passenger habits, ways of life, and communities as by virtue of thickening the medium through which passengers must pass, making it dense, impregnable, and visible.

Differently put, the passages of passengers are conditional, but, at the extreme, their conditionality passes into impassibility. Our passports are the things that embody this conditionality, the necessary but—in and of themselves—insufficient prerequisites for being granted passage within and between states. Actually, passports are an invention of Johann Gottlieb Fichte, a German philosopher, whose life spanned the end of the eighteenth and the beginning of the nineteenth centuries. In his *Foundations of Natural Right*, Fichte recommends the use of passport prototypes in a well-policed state, where "the principal maxim" is that "*every citizen must be readily identifiable, wherever necessary, as this or that particular person. . . .* Everyone must always carry an identity card [*Pass*] with him, issued by the nearest authority and containing a precise description of his person; this applies to everyone, regardless of class or rank. Since merely verbal

The passages of passengers are conditional, but, at the extreme, their conditionality passes into impassibility.

descriptions always remain ambiguous, it might be good if important persons (who therefore can afford it as well) were to carry accurate portraits in their identity cards, rather than descriptions."[3] For Fichte, easy police identification via a passport (and now also through the techno-gaze of CCTV cameras) should be able to freeze passenger flows whenever the need arises. This potential stoppage is a condition of and an instrument for conditioning people's movements.

What the equivalence of passing and passing through teaches us is that, as passengers, we never pass through a vacuum. Nor are we a vacuum moving in vacuum—disembodied minds crisscrossing the earth, the sea, and the skies, unencumbered with fragile bodies that are prone to get sick and that are used to life in certain climates and time zones. The thickness and nontransparency of the medium, with which we've gotten reacquainted in a pandemic state, are the thickness and nontransparency of materiality, of the physicality of existence. The point is to remember this crucial lesson even when everything is functioning smoothly and seamlessly once again: to be or to become passengers mindful of the constraints on our passengerhood. To live with the appreciation of the real possibility that *we might not pass*.

stage of its development. Despite not being on a train or aboard a plane, in a bus or a subway car, we retain a passenger attitude to places, each of them potentially available for passing through and for leaving behind, for geolocation or for digital identification on Google Earth.

With the Midas touch of our passenger space-consciousness, we turn each place into a *here* that is already *there*, before, after, and while we pass through it. As Hegel writes: "The Here is not yet place, but only the possibility of Place; the Heres are completely the same, [forming] this abstract plurality without real interruption or limit."[1] For a passenger concerned with the most efficient way of getting somewhere, there are no places—just "the possibility of Place," as Hegel has it. It is, moreover, a possibility that never comes to fruition, because the destination will be a waypoint for yet another *here* that is a *there*. Our biggest problem is not the absence of possibilities, but infinite possibilities that paralyze us in the midst of an "abstract plurality without real interruption or limit." Weird as this may sound, paralysis does not mean stoppage and immobility here (in this kaleidoscopic plurality of *here*s). It befalls us, instead, in the experience of constant dislocation, in movement without respite, as though we were stuck in a traffic jam of gargantuan proportions during rush hour that is all the hours.

The spatial experience of human passengers is but an exaggerated version of the animal sense of place. Nonsessile animals, by definition, do not stay in the same place; they move from spot to spot, as slowly as a snail or as fast as a cheetah. The *here* of such an animal continually changes, with the effect that, dialectically speaking, the truth of the *here* is that it is *no longer here*, or, simply, *not-here* but *already over there*. Hegel, again: "I, *this* 'I,' see the tree and assert that 'Here' is a tree; but another 'I' [which may be me, myself, at another moment in time, MM] sees the house and maintains that 'Here' is not a tree but a house instead. Both truths have the same authentication [. . .], but the one truth vanishes in the other."[2] And how much more quickly is the *here* that is a tree replaced by another *here* that is a house during our travels! With the same velocity, the truth of the first assertion vanishes in the truth of the second, which vanishes in the truth of the third . . . The truth of the *here* evanesces in the maelstrom of these disappearances. The passenger sense of places is their replacement by other places.

Hold on a moment. Let's go (drive, sail, fly . . .) back to the tree, which has all of a sudden sprouted in Hegel's example of the initial *here*. We've said that the passenger experience of space is an exaggeration of animal experience. But plants are not here in the same way that a house is here. They are also living beings and, as such, they should have a living relation to the places they inhabit.

Although it is incredibly difficult to imagine the world from the perspective of a plant, we can venture a more or less educated guess about this perspective. A tree, rooted in the site where it grows, does not physically negate its *here* by relocating to another *here*. It grows, changes, and decays with the *here* that it is. The *here* of a tree is not monotonously the same; it extends and contracts, branches out and flourishes, crumbles to the earth and evaporates into the atmosphere together with parts of the tree itself. Who or what is here—in front of, on, below, above, or around—the tree also varies: a flock of birds, chirping in its crown; orchard bees and hoverflies, visiting its blossoms in the spring; fungi and bacteria creating symbiotic relations with its roots; you and I standing before it when we are not on trains, buses, or planes. If plants, and especially trees, draw us toward themselves as though they were green magnets, that is because they awaken in us a faint memory of calm without stagnation, of tenacious energy that has nothing in common with the to-and-fro sustaining our illusion of bustling activity.

Are plants the exemplary nonpassengers, then? Not really. Their seeds, spores, and pollen catch a ride on airflows and in the intestines of the rodents or birds who ingest them, on butterfly wings and a bee's hind legs. These vegetal genetic materials are highly mobile, migratory, diasporic (*diaspora* originally meant "the scattering of the seed"). Before any other conceivable characterization, they are unmistakably, quintessentially, passengers. Just think of their togetherness and separation, the randomness of their reproductive trajectories and compartmentalization according to the species of pollinators they attract, the passivity of their being carried and the fertilizing activity this passive carriage facilitates. Plus, there is the matter of the unnoticed, unintended excess that vegetal passengers constitute with regard to their elemental and biological conveyances. Who are we to deny that "perhaps, plants dream up their elsewhere in this throw of the dice" that is the release of pollen, spores, or seeds, as I speculate in my *Grafts*?[3]

Turning the human-centered perspective around, we should assert that it is not parts of plants that are passengers like us, but, vice versa, we are passengers like them. Vegetal and animal migrations had occurred long before the evolutionary emergence of *Homo sapiens sapiens*. Our passenger routines, among many other modes of conduct and organization, are mimetic: they imitate the behavior of nonhuman forms of life and their respective relations to space. The French origin of the word *passenger* is indicative of this imitation. According to the Littré dictionary, the noun and the adjective *passager* are tied to *oiseaux passagers*, birds of passage, or migratory birds. It signifies fleetingness, impermanence, a short duration, "being in a place merely in passing" ("*Un passager, un homme qui n'est dans un lieu qu'en passant*: a passenger, a man who is in a place merely in passing"). A passenger does the opposite of dwelling in or inhabiting a place and is akin to migratory birds, who move between habitats and between climates with the onset of cooler weather. But our passengerhood, unlike that of birds, is ideally free of spatial (geographic) and temporal (seasonal) constraints, a freedom that is nevertheless tested by border authorities, ticket prices, pandemics, and anthropogenic climate change.

The disappearance of the *here* gains momentum. Compared to animals and parts of plants, the quantitative change in the speed and frequency with which we pass through places, leaving them behind, is so significant that it triggers a qualitative alteration in our relation to place and to space. If nothing and no one is *right here*, then there is no *over there* either; following Hegel, the truth of every *here* is its negation in a *not-here*, and, if the *here* is annihilated, so is the *there* set over and against it. The coordinates of experienced space collapse. If what remains of places is a bunch of points of passage, transit, transition, or transfer stations, then, as passengers passing through them, we hurry from nowhere to nowhere. Our travels and travails widen and maintain the cleft between the former nowhere and the latter. We hope that, in this way, on account of this widening, the one will not crush into the other, wiping us off the face of the earth.

In the ceaseless mobility of passenger societies, places neither preexist nor survive our passing through them. A place as a point of passage receives its raison d'être, as much as its definiteness, from the act of passing through it. Passenger places are short-lived flashes, illuminating for an instant a given point in the otherwise homogeneous space and then swishing back into obscurity. It may seem that some places are permanently aglow; in cities that never sleep, it is always daytime. In effect, the stability of the present (not least of the presence of places) is guaranteed by the permanent flux of those who pass through a site. The new navels of the world, megalopolises are enormous passenger hubs, living off the flows of people, goods, and capital that inundate them, often to the detriment of birds, marine life, and other animals. Their stability is, however, self-undermining: the more passengers move through a place, keeping it in existence by virtue of their movement, the less likely it is to come back into being after the streams of people, goods, and emissions passing through it have devastated it environmentally, physically, and metaphysically.

So entrenched is the logic of places as points of passage that tourists, travelers, and even residents are now passengerish. The only meaningful distinction between these groups is based on how long it takes them to pass through a place, including the place called home. With this logic expanded to the planetary scale, we contend that we are all passengers on Spaceship Earth, carrying us through space and time. The planet turns into a means of transport, its fragile ecosystems—the crew and the supplies guaranteeing that our needs are met for the duration of the orbital journey from nowhere to nowhere. Finally, the proposals that are now gaining steam for humanity to evolve into an interplanetary species call for the conversion of planet Earth into a mere waypoint in a cosmic passenger society. Stripped of its romantic trappings, the unadorned idea behind these recommendations is that—rather than regions, countries, or continents—planets at different stages of despoiling would be stopover habitats for the human, or posthuman, migratory birds.

Although we have contemplated the places passengers pass through, we have not yet given enough thought to the interiors of our means of transport. Coming onboard, passengers must occupy their places on a bus, a tram, a ship, or a plane to commence their journeys. The inner organization of public transports is determined, precisely, by the placement of passengers and of their luggage. At the degree zero of a *here* that is moving past and nullifying the rest of what used to be *here*, "place" is an act before it is a noun. Assigned and taken by beings animate and inanimate, as the case may be, it is a derivative of the verb *to place*, just as time is secondary with respect to *timing*. The competing considerations in the allocation of passenger places are efficiency and the luxury of ample personal space. Different classes of passengers are given their respective placements depending on where they fall in the spectrum of options situated between these two extremes. But once class differences are not a factor in the internal organization of space on a means of transport, discomfort and overcrowding prevail, as in the Tokyo subway during rush hour.

In a paradox characteristic of our day and age, the rigidity and stability of placements inside boats, buses, trains, or planes coincide with the unsettlement and destabilization of the places outside, through which passengers pass. The sense of place now emanates from unsettlement and displacement: of passengers and the means of transport that carry and ferry us; of the locales we travel through and change by polluting them with noise and carbon emissions; of dwelling,

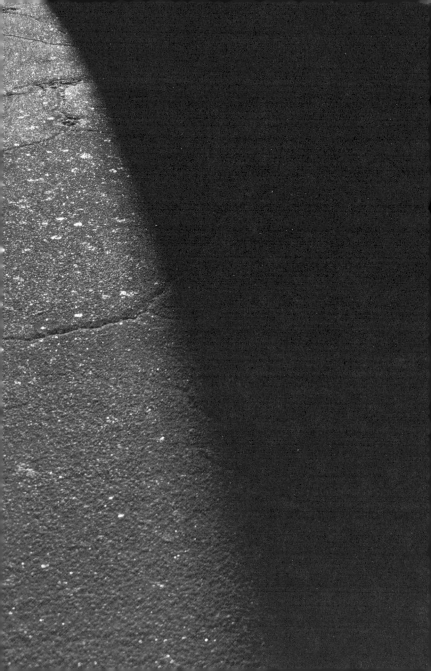

Stop no. 4: Existence

If we are to believe a nearly unanimous chorus of commentators, modern philosophy begins in the exact moment when, seated by the fireplace in his study, French philosopher René Descartes questions his own existence and that of the outside world. Descartes opens his first meditation with a number of doubts, sending a series of shudders through the certainty "that I am now here, sitting by the fire, wrapped in a warm winter gown, handling this paper, and suchlike."[1] "That I am now here": this phrase rings alarm bells for us, who have witnessed the dissipation of *here* in the space-consciousness and of *now* in the time-consciousness of passengers. As a passenger, I am already not here and not now, in the here-and-now of my trip. So, how do things stand with "I am," the *sum* in Descartes's famous *cogito ergo sum*, "I think, therefore, I am"?

I am a passenger: I am in a passage and in passing, *en passant*, fleetingly. I both am and am not at one and the same time, the time that shies away from the fixed instant of a *now*. I am: always on the verge of not being, of having passed, of having passed away, no longer keeping open the cleft between nowhere and nowhere. Without a *why*, I am a passenger irrespective of the purpose of my trip, the usual *business or pleasure?* And I exist also, for the most part, without asking myself *what for?* When and where I am are not queries that are somehow tangential, subordinate to who or what I am; they define and perennially redefine me. In transit. Between departure and arrival, which is, at bottom, a nonarrival, to the extent that it is transformed into yet another point of departure.

What formal logic sees as inadmissible contradictions—I am and am not; both here and not here, now and not now—are the indicators of existential intensity and vigor. Existence is not static; to resort to Heidegger's word, it is ecstatic, standing outside itself in itself. Differently put, existence is exitence, a departure from the fortress of identity. Exiting oneself, one exists as an I.

Existence is exitence, a departure from the fortress of identity. Exiting oneself, one exists as an I.

(Picture the EXIT signs that light up on a plane with an S slotted between the I and the T. With this alternative spelling, at takeoff and landing, you would be urged to EXIST, especially in emergency situations.)

It is a tall order to interpret existence existentially, not metaphysically, keeping exitence in play. A passenger in metaphysical philosophy and in our everyday thinking remains the same person at point A, B, and at all the points in-between. It seems a matter of common sense that those who pass through the world do not themselves pass, that they stay the same at every step of the way. Existentially (or exitentially) understood, though, passengers pass along with the world, surpassing themselves time and again, even if, in a state of boredom, they feel that nothing is happening, nothing is changing. An instant is a gap for exiting the stronghold of your identity and, therefore, for existing, for being otherwise than you have been or than you are: no longer "one," but "I-myself," where the I does not coincide with myself. Some instants are tiny windows and escape hatches, others are turnstiles, still others are wide-open gates. In the condition of passengerhood, they fly by us in a rapid succession, as fast as (if not faster than) the changing landscape. Our challenge is to catch up with an instant that is just right, so that we would be able to exit ourselves through it. *Mind the gap*, indeed!

(Tourists quit themselves, but they keep returning in an uninterrupted rotation, orbiting themselves as they move through the sites they tour and barely notice. Before fulfilling its stated purpose, the selfie stick works as the radius of that intimate touristy circle.)

To return not to ourselves but to Descartes, I wonder what the French philosopher would have thought about his outfit, his hands, and the paper before him were they to have appeared not in the flickering glow of the fire burning in his fireplace but in the beam of a reading light above his plane seat, in the total illumination of an airport terminal, or in the fitful flares of tunnel lights streaking past the window of a subway train flooded with light from within. After all, when and where philosophy takes place is not an incidental factor; when and where I am are not peripheral to my identity. Radical as his doubt may have been, Descartes is at home, *chez soi*, not on the road, where the stable reality he is suspicious about shows no signs of stability whatsoever. So much so that he is at home in doubt itself, which he domesticates and eventually disbands in the certainty of the *cogito*, of indubitability based on the fact that someone—an I, actually indistinguishable from "one"—is thinking it.

These musings raise serious questions. Does existence require physical exitence? If yes, how far from home? Or should we forget all about home and become nomadic in order to exist "authentically," genuinely?

Judged by the criterion of distancing from home and of embracing nomadism, traditional philosophers hardly existed. Descartes, to his credit, traveled to Sweden, where he taught Queen Christina philosophy and where he died after catching pneumonia as a consequence of giving his lessons at 5:00 a.m. in wintertime. Immanuel Kant had famously never left his native Königsberg, a city that has itself left Prussia/Germany after World War II and is now known as the Russian Kaliningrad. Along with Königsberg, political and geographical regions affected by wars or climate change are history's passengers. Vitoria-Gasteiz, the city where I am jotting down these lines, includes its itinerary and destination in a double, hyphenated name—in part Spanish, in part Basque (*vitoria* means "victory," referring to Wellington's victory over the Napoleonic forces in 1813, while *gasteiz* signifies "young," from the

Basque word *gaztea*). It is not necessary to leave a place behind for existence to reach a high pitch of intensity: places can grow unhomely all by themselves or as a result of our changing attitudes toward them. Nomadism is not propitious to existence, because, in its tireless roaming, there is nowhere to disembark, no frictions or resistances conducive to movement, nothing to exit, no home, and no self—not even a one-self—to push off from.

As passengers, then, we give a spatial expression to the exitence of existence. We can also take leave of ourselves and of where we are at the moment in thought, in imagination, in our dreams. These means of psychological transport are no less efficient than a train or a plane. It follows that, dreaming, imagining, and thinking aboard, we escalate the exitence of existence, scrambling its spatial and psychic registers. Every bus ride is an allegory of reverie; to fantasize on a bus is to deliver oneself to existence raised to the power of two.

The exits at the heart of existence reveal that to exist is to retreat from something or someone, notably from certain versions of oneself and, at the extreme, from oneself as a whole. Death shapes the horizon of finite life. *Exit stage left* (though not always by breaking the glass, pulling the handle, and pushing the emergency door or window wide open). But, while our future Exit from life towers—consciously or not—over the living of this life, the exits that instigate existence refer to the past, to all the apparently dynamic conveyances and relations, to all the presumably stationary places and identities, we leave behind. As exitence, the character of existence is Janus-faced: prospective and retrospective, forward- and backward-looking. And it could well be that all the exits we make on a daily (and nightly) basis, however insignificant, amount to practicing the big Exit that awaits us or that we await, the Exit at which we await ourselves, at the final stop of existence.

More globally, you might be interested in why the world exists. Why is there something rather than nothing? A child's curiosity is a precious trait that we let go of too easily in adult life. Awakening our inner child, we might marvel and wonder about the existence of beings as diverse as humans and rocks, rivers and computers, fish and buildings, and . . . Should we not be enraptured by existence, in its amazing array of variations, without steering everything to the terminal and the terminus of the subject, of the I who thinks, who senses and makes sense, who dies or awaits death?

For passengers, existence is split roughly between the outside world and the inner realm. Such splitting is typical of both philosophical and colloquial approaches to this theme. The caveat is that "the inner realm" of passenger experience does not stand (only) for the hidden sphere of our thoughts, fears and aspirations, desires and inclinations; it is (also) an aircraft cabin or a railcar, the salon of a tram or a bus. The two spatial domains seem to obey different, even diametrically opposed, laws. Inside, we feel stability, uninterrupted by the rhythmic swaying of the moving conveyance and the roar of its engines relegated to the auditory background as white noise. Outside, the world appears to be a blur, when we travel through it at high speed, or a gradually passing procession of the more or less individuated shapes, colors, and textures when we move through it at a slower pace. At times, what is unfolding behind the window ceases to exist; at other times, with our gazes wandering, lost in the outside expanses, the mobile cocoon of the means of transport disappears in its naturalization, in its being experienced as an extension of our biological bodies, as second nature or techno-skin.

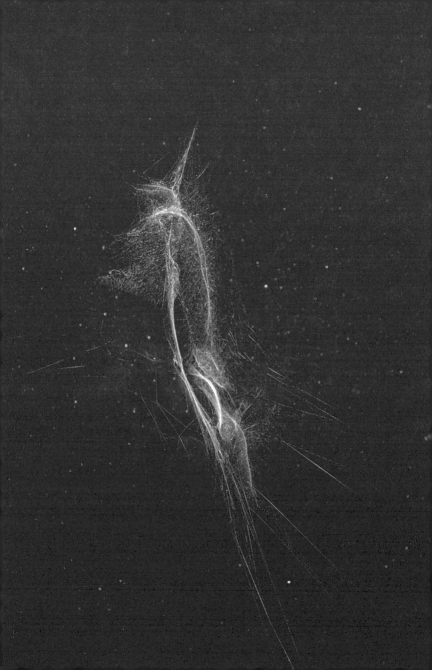

Detour no. 2: Passengers, Hollywood Style

In the midst of superhero glamor, does Hollywood ever turn to mundane passenger experience?

Well, the setting for the film *Passengers*, directed by Morten Tyldum and released in 2016, is not a bus or a run-of-the-mill cruise ship, but the spacecraft *Avalon*, carrying thousands of hibernating people to a faraway planet. Since the journey takes 120 years, it is essential that passengers remain asleep almost up until their arrival at Homestead II. Yet, in the aftermath of a technical failure caused by the collision of the spaceship with an asteroid, one of the passengers, James Preston (Chris Pratt), awakens only thirty years into the trip. Lonely, he rouses a fellow passenger, Aurora Lane (Jennifer Lawrence), with whom he eventually resolves the spacecraft's malfunctions and leads a full life aboard the *Avalon*. After the rest of the passengers shake off more than a century of sleep in the orbit of Homestead II (which is eerily similar to our Earth), they discover aboard a paradisiac place filled with vegetation and birds, along with Lane's diary, in which she writes: "A lot happened while you slept. A friend once said: 'You can't get so hung up on where you'd rather be that you forget to make the most of where you are.' We got lost along the way. But we found each other. And we made a life, a beautiful life, together."

Rehearsing a number of archetypal Western narratives—from the creation of Adam and Eve to Robinson Crusoe and Sleeping Beauty—in a futuristic setting, *Passengers* brings something new into them. The genuine novelty of the film is in how it slots a myth of the origin into the middle of a journey, giving a literal twist to the interpretation to *inter*planetary life. A trip that exceeds the span of a human life, which is not spent in hibernation, means that the destination will never be reached and that life in a suspended, in-between condition is all there is. The destination is unattainable, as is the origin, which coincides with an awakening in the middle of a journey, encompassing and surpassing a lifetime.

A trip that exceeds the span of a human life means that the destination will never be reached and that life in a suspended, in-between condition is all there is.

The physical process of waking up has reliably provided the template for spiritual and rational rebirth and awakening, be it in the context of conversion and faith, the enlightenment and the technoscientific outlook, or, more recently and ironically, becoming "woke," superficially aware of the problems of social and racial justice. As soon as, by fluke, James discovers that he is the only person not submerged in deep slumber among the passengers and crew of the *Avalon*, he becomes the first to attain passenger experience. That is his enlightenment. Plainly put, James comes to experience himself as a passenger, something that others, hibernating in their pods, do not feel about themselves. In contrast to the anaesthetized state of his fellow space travelers, he finds *himself*, getting reacquainted with himself in the middle of a journey that will never end (at least for him): given the timeframe of the trip to Homestead II, he knows that he will not make it to the other planet alive. Henceforth, the horizon of death, as opposed to that of arrival, confers meaning onto his vigil aboard the *Avalon*.

James is alone in the world, like Adam before the creation of Eve or Crusoe before he meets Friday. His awakening is unreal, because he has no one to share it with: the bartender Arthur, whom he mistakes for a human, turns out to be an android. (By the way, the name of the bartender is yet another pointer as to the meaning of this Hollywood parable: Avalon is a utopian island of old Arthurian legends, the place where the sword Excalibur was forged.) To give a stamp of reality to his newly found passenger experience, James needs another human being, which is why he wakes up Aurora.

In a reversal of the story of Sleeping Beauty, who is resuscitated with a kiss, Aurora rises from her slumber to death. More exactly, she awakens to the intermediacy of life, right where she is (on a starship, which is something like an island floating through space, or an isolated Edenic garden), not where she'd rather be (on Earth 2.0). But Aurora is much more than an object of rescue or damnation, and also more than a mirror, in which James can seek the confirmation of his own newly discovered existence. A pivotal scene in the movie is one where the couple find out that Autodoc—an automated scanning, diagnostic, and medical treatment area on the spaceship—can serve as a hibernation pod for one person. By making the choice not to use it for herself, Aurora asserts her will, retroactively authorizing her unchosen awakening. It is in this precise moment that she gains access to passenger experience, to existence in the midst of a journey that, for her as well, will never come to a close.

What, then, is "the beautiful life" Aurora claims that she and James made for themselves? It is a life lived in the shadow of death, which one cannot evade, the life marked by nonarrival or nonfruition and imbued with its deepest meaning through its finitude. Some might draw solace from the act of bringing children into the world as younger versions of themselves and as their replacements. But the final shots of *Passenger* evince something else: the legacy of Aurora and James is a livable environment filled with plant and animal life, a veritable Paradise planted not by God in the driver's seat of creation, but by the self-conscious passengers of existence. The future generation is not altogether absent from the picture, either; it comprises all the fellow passengers, who shake off their hibernation at the appointed time before the starship's landing on Homestead II. Those who watch attentively will spot a subtle Hollywood rejoinder to the ideology of plunder and colonialism blown to cosmic proportions in the current advocacy of humanity as an interplanetary species. Instead of looking for another Earth to pillage and strip of its resources, we should be caring for and cultivating the here-and-now, even if this here-and-now is itself moving, changing, evanescing, and perhaps reappearing again.

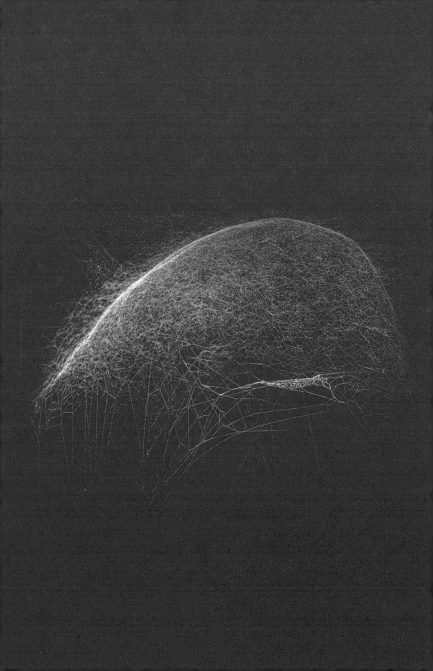

Stop no. 5: Transport

. . . I am carried away somewhere. By endless torrents of words and images, thoughts and intuitions hauling other images and thoughts in a seemingly unending train that I ride and that I am. Unless it is this train that rides through me . . . The elusive *somewhere* appears to be beyond myself, lying across a gulf, which I may never traverse and which I traverse without fail whenever I am carried along in this way. I am transported, I transport myself, and I am the means of transport: passenger and cargo, train and conductor. There is no communication without such transport, no address, no receiving messages—new or old, the news or the olds (which is how news reach us in the twenty-first century)—from other human beings and from the world at large, without edging close to the outer limits of myself and leaping across an abyss. Assuming

I am transported, I transport myself, and I am the means of transport: passenger and cargo, train and conductor.

that on the other side something or someone directs themself or itself toward me, there is also a chance of encountering the other in a head-on collision, a train wreck of "successful" communication, an act of transport that actually reaches its destination.

***

Our transportation systems draw an important distinction between cargo and passenger vessels or vehicles: barges and cruise ships or ocean liners, freighters and airliners, freight and passenger trains. (Smaller and more local, buses, trams, and taxies are passenger means of transport that do not operate with this distinction in mind.) The two types of transport correspond neatly to the philosophical division between subject and object, the *who* and the *what*. But are things so clear-cut? For one, the mobility of goods and people in the interest of economic growth and free trade levels the subject–object division to the extent that both its constituents are objects for capital. For another, not only do passengers travel with their luggage next to them or in the hold compartment, but, as already mentioned, they also carry other barely visible or invisible passengers and loads on and in them. Instead of *who is who?* and *what is what?*, the relevant questions of a passenger society and thinking are *who carries what?* and *what carries whom?*

Transported by the means of transport, we ourselves are the vehicles for microscopic nonhuman passengers, such as viruses and bacteria. We smuggle aboard the psychological and ideational luggage that, itself weightless, accompanies us everywhere. As psychophysical units, embodied minds and mindful bodies, each of us is two: a *who* and a *what*. Where is the transporting and the transported here? Who *and* what are passengers, both carried by and carrying their bodies that, if need be, are assisted by other medical or technical devices?

Each of us is a small-scale transportation system with hybridized passenger and hold compartments, circulating in public transit and transportation networks worldwide: a transported and transporting microcosm in a transported and transporting macrocosm. But it is not enough to contemplate the passive and the active dynamics of carrying to get a hang of the meaning of transportation. Condensed in this term is the promise that something or someone would be carried beyond what is here—despite the devastation of every *here*—across the chasm separating this side from the other. Transportation spans two sides, or two shores, more focused on these sides or shores themselves than on what stretches between them. Brimming with sunny optimism, transportation gives us the assurance (the pledge, really) that what lies beyond is reachable, that the beyond has been and will be reached.

Besides the word *transportation*, we stumble upon *trans-* in transatlantic flights and the Trans-Siberian Railway, while another Latin prefix *inter-* jumps at us from the routes and companies of intercity buses and trains or international travel. With an eye trained over years of philosophical practice to spot minor and apparently inconsequential differences, I have become transfixed (yet another *trans-* or trance) by this distinction. I am further convinced that, in the competition between *across* and *between*, we are facing yet another facet of the dialectic of passengerhood. How so?

What presents itself to us as a slight linguistic variation is, in effect, a sea change in the view of the same trip from the perspectives of departure and destination or from the middle of having already departed but not yet arrived. The *trans-* of transport and of continental, oceanic, and other journeys across geographically vast areas leaps over the enormous expanses it spans. The *inter-* of international travel and intercity trips emphasizes the stretch in-between. Traversal and suspension, passing through and failing to pass, arrival and nonarrival, fulfillment and nonfulfillment: in its spatiotemporal dimension, passenger experience is, like passenger society, possible only thanks to the indissoluble tensions created by these poles.

Recall how, in discussing the time of passengers, I asked you to concentrate on the excluded part—the middle, akin to this very clarification locked between two dashes—and to reconstruct beginnings and ends from what lies between them. To throw space into the mix, you might freeze the frame and observe yourself from the vantage of your departure, looking forward to your journey and arrival; from your travels themselves, without dwelling on the moment of departure or anticipating that of arrival; and from the instant of arrival, glancing back at your departure and the rest of the voyage. Passenger experience consists of these three imperfectly overlapping frames, a 3D vision in space and time.

The reason why the structure of passenger experience is dialectical is that, though they go together, *across* and *between* also cancel each other out. On the two sides spanned by the *trans-* of transportation, the transported is not yet or no longer a passenger; in the middle stretch of the *inter-*, passengers are traveling without either the foundational security of the beginning or the certainty of arrival at the end. The starting and the terminal points are connected by the line of the itinerary passing between them, the line that is both their continuation and interruption. In the same way, a relation is made of the parties to a relation and the task of relating that takes the participants to the furthest limits, beyond their isolated selves. Thinking of relations, we usually imagine what lies *across* the gulf separating each party from the other and do not bother with everything happening *between* them. Our passenger experience enacts the drama of relation each time we board a bus, travel on a transcontinental flight, or arrive at a train station, marking the end of our journey.

***

I am carried away, beyond myself. Before I have the other side in view and after I reach it (assuming that I do), the carrying, the transporting, is the only reality I have access to. I am a passenger before and after I am a passenger. I ship myself off. Is my body a shipping container for the mind? Or is the mind the carrier of the body in this stretch of what lies in-between, which I call *my life*? Who transports what? What transports whom?

***

Speaking of transport, we unfailingly add "means of" before this word. The idea that whatever carries us, our wares, or natural raw materials is the means takes it as given that transportation is the end goal. But it is, in turn, the means for something else (travel for leisure or work, trade in goods, and the like), which is the means for yet another thing, and so on, and so on. Though servicing fixed routes or running along predefined tracks, means of transport are, in fact, the embodiments of means without ends: without a fixed purpose and endless, infinite, lacking closure in the grid they form.

The expression itself razes all variations among vehicles and vessels, buses and trains, ships and planes.

Faster or slower, flying or driving, sailing or running along a track, all means of transport are equal in their capacity as instruments. Their indifference and non-differentiation perfectly matches the nihilistic attitude that is so rampant today, a nonchalant shoulder shrug or an apathetic *whatever*, mouthed half-audibly. Our means of transport are the material infrastructure for shuttling pure means that include us, ourselves, in the role of passengers eager to get somewhere, anywhere, so long as we are there on time.

One of the latest twists on the pure means (of transport) is the trend of the "flights to nowhere" that started in 2020 first in Australia and later in Taiwan.[1] These flights circle, for hours on end, over national territory only to return to the airport, from which they departed. Whom or what do they transport? Is there anything or anyone left either across or between the distances they span? The physical circle they complete is also metaphysical: pure means are reworked into the ends in themselves. Flights and cruises to nowhere are encrusted into another circle still—that of capital accumulation, in which financial means are the ends, largely indifferent to the commodities that proliferate as their side effect.

Things could have been different. Transport hubs, such as seaports, airports, or train stations, could have been portals, gateways to other worlds. Not to the worlds of an exoticized other, but to those where the transported are othered, put in question, compelled to abandon the comfort zone of entrenched mental schemes and prejudices.

In a similar vein, we may interpret afresh the religious and revolutionary concept of *the world to come*. Try reading this expression hyperliterally. The world to come means that another world is rushing toward us, is coming, arriving at our doorstep, transporting us elsewhere without the interference of any conventional means of transport. It is not we who, reaching another world, breach its boundaries and intrude into its domain; the coming world itself infringes on the territory of this world, surprising the established order of existence. It comes from the future as a derailed train, which, in fact, runs along a previously unseen track, from the to-come that catches up with us before we can grasp, contain, and master it.

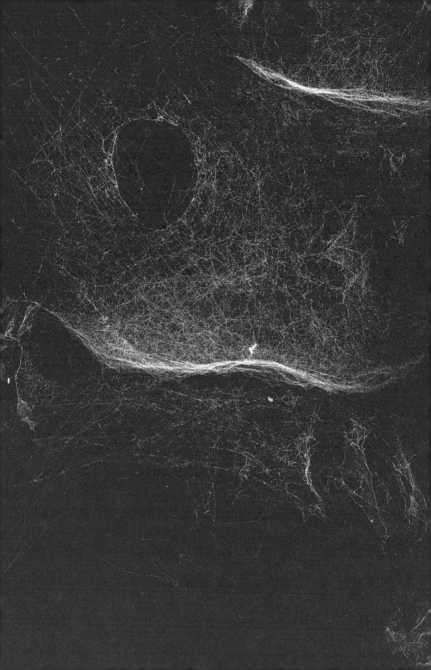

Stop no. 6: Metaphor

Metaphor is a unique means of transport. As a matter of fact, the word *metaphor* says, precisely, *transport*— only in Greek, instead of Latin. Metaphors are the vessels of meaning that let it swiftly glide on the waters of sense. More often than not, they stand in sharp contrast to literalness, which allegedly denotes the fixity of meaning, its inability to travel anywhere beyond the site of its enunciation or inscription. The literal sticks to the bareness of what is expressed, to the self-proclaimed basic and original truth of expression; the metaphoric passes from a certain kind of object or idea to ideas and objects of a different kind, from one order of meaning to another.

I've always had strong doubts about the wisdom and the plausibility of hard and fast distinctions between literalness and metaphoricity. Would these distinctions themselves be literal or metaphoric? Further, to arrest meaning in its literal straitjacket is to interfere with its vital operations that depend on its instability and motility. Meaning-making only works if, addressed to others, the message travels, changing hands, mutating, inviting fresh interpretations and modes of reception at each stop along its itinerary. Metaphoric drift may be inseparable from this dynamism, which I earlier called "our sense of sense, the paradigm of meaning in perpetual motion." For its part, a strict opposition between the literal and the metaphoric rehashes the philosophical mind/body split, with the proviso that, in this instance, one's preference goes to the embodied and the concrete at the expense of metaphor taken as mere whim, a caprice of the imagination.

Are the passengers we have been musing about metaphorical? Yes and no. The figure of the passenger includes you and me in our daily routines of moving about and relating to the world. But, in so doing, this figure reaches beyond the actual instances of train rides or commercial flights to an existential predicament, in which we are accustomed to perceive reality, to experience time, places, and ourselves as though we have never gotten off the train nor deplaned. The transfer of a passenger mindset to other situations in life that, on the face of things, have nothing in common with means of transport slots it between literal and metaphoric significations. If, from time to time, we are all passengers, and if we unconsciously play the role of passengers both before and after we get on or off the proverbial bus, then the register of such thinking is mixed: literal-metaphorical or metaphorico-literal.

Much of my work has occupied the gray (what a misnomer! anything but gray, it is vibrant and multicolored) area between literalness and metaphoricity. From dust to fire, from plants to the dump, I have sought figures of thought and existence, through which the categories of the old metaphysical philosophy could be sifted and transformed beyond recognition. Figuration is what abstract modes of cogitation are allergic to; the thrust of abstraction may be defined as that of a generalized un- or disfiguration. As far as the philosophy that prides itself on its strict adherence to the analytic method is concerned, figuration is an anachronistic vestige of "nonscientific" thought that does not lend itself fully to operationalization or translation into logical formulae and algorithms. But what remains without figures? What is there to be discerned

A little like dust, passengers gather temporarily in haphazard social formations only to disperse again.

Passengerhood is, therefore, not *just* a metaphor, nor is it a purely literal condition of being a passenger. It is *passing through what, itself, passes by and away*. Modern means of transport that massify passenger experience or nonexperience parachute us right to the palpitating heart of modernity, which, more than life in the fast lane, is the accelerating movement of passing that leaves us with no time to acknowledge what or who has passed, whom or what we have passed. Passenger transports are metaphors in the most literal sense of ferrying across. Metaphors are the most literal vehicles for the passages of meaning.

Traditionally, metaphors belonged under the heading of rhetoric. It was not until the nineteenth century's Romantic opposition to Classicism that they gained significance beyond the study of the art of speaking and writing. In the first half of the twentieth century, Ivor Armstrong Richards, the British literary critic who stood at the origins of the formalist movement in literary theory called New Criticism, advocated a substantial broadening of metaphor's scope. In his Mary Flexner Lectures on the Humanities, which he delivered at Bryn Mawr College in 1936, Richards argued: "*Thought* is metaphoric, and proceeds by comparison, and the metaphors of language derive therefrom. To improve the theory of metaphor we must remember this."[1] The "shifting and displacement of words" in metaphoric expressions is but the tip of the iceberg that is the disquietude of thought, its indefatigable shuttling back and forth in comparisons, assessments, and judgments. Thoroughly metaphoric, thought *is* passengerhood, inasmuch as, hugging two shores or two sides, it is alive both to these terms of comparison and to the gulf that persists between them.

What Richards's uncompromising stance indicates is that metaphor is not a superfluous element of language, ornamental at best, duplicitous at worst. It is indispensable to the processes of thinking. In view of this maximalist theory of metaphor, we would do well to examine some of the metaphors organizing our approach to the figure of passengers, mindful of the metaphoric nature of thinking as an ethereal means of transport.

If you say that you are "in the driver's seat," you imply that you are the one in charge of a situation. This is the opposite of occupying a passenger seat and being driven without having your hands on the wheel. As we have seen, however, in their privileged passivity, passengers may be more active than the driver. The metaphor is self-undermining: our depreciation of the passenger position covers over its centrality in contemporary society and, indeed, its formative influence on the experiences of place, time, and the world.

At the more literal end of the spectrum, "backseat drivers" contest the actual driver's position of control by commenting on the latter's actions and giving annoying sets of instruction. Here, a passenger assumes the role of the driver in spite of staying put in a passenger seat, combining the passivity of being driven along with the active determination of the route and conduct. The expression is widely applicable outside the field of transport, as well: it hints at the (oft-times groundless) assertion of one's superior knowledge and expert authority in the absence of hands-on engagement with the practical task.

In the field of psychology, the "Passengers on the Bus" metaphor is part of the acceptance and commitment therapy (ACT), developed by the American psychologist Steven Hayes. Here, the person in therapy is compared to a bus driver, whose thoughts, memories, and emotional states are so many passengers taking a ride on the bus. Some of the passengers start threatening the driver, at which point secret deals are made to placate the unruly bus riders so that they do not come to the front of the bus and take it over. To break harmful psychological dynamics, Hayes insists, one ought to remember who is in the driver's seat: "The driver (you) has control of the bus, but you trade away the control in these secret deals with the passengers. In other words, by trying to get control, you've actually given up control!"[2] Since the premise of ACT is a strict division of labor between the conscious subject (the driver) and unconscious affects and thoughts (passengers), the goal is to reestablish control by putting the driver back in the driver's seat, so to speak. But are passengers in a purely passive position, especially in this metaphoric rendition of psychic life? Is repression (Hayes's "secret deals") lifted the moment conscious life asserts its imaginary control over the unconscious? Is repression not, on the contrary, strengthened, its mechanisms further obfuscated, in mental exercises, such as "Passengers on the Bus"?

Laying insidious influences on metaphoric passengers is also common in environmental studies. In their recent work on the expansion of blue catfish populations in mid-Atlantic waters, Donald Orth, Joseph

Schmitt, and Corbin Hilling analyze scientific, managerial, and media discourses about invasive species. They suggest replacing aggressive, militaristic metaphors prevalent with regard to blue catfish with those that "refer to introduced species as passengers, backseat drivers, and drivers of ecosystem degradation."[3] The basic idea is that nonnative species are passengers who propagate having caught a ride on changing environmental conditions, not the drivers (or the causes) of adverse ecological effects. Besides a passivity-laden notion of ecological passengers, at issue in the proposed metaphoric revision is the reassignment of responsibilities: passengers are not responsible for the cumulative consequences of their actions; the onus is on the driver. But what if we transpose this conclusion from the metaphoric to the literal register? Is a pilot or a driver assigned a particular route more responsible for adverse ecological effects than the passengers who take a highly polluting plane or bus? Just as the distribution of active and passive attitudes has turned out to be very complex, so the dividing lines between culpability and innocence are blurred whenever passengers are involved, not least in the guise of a metaphor.

Connection/Transfer: Passages

We are in the middle of the book, which is not necessarily its physical halfway mark, in the middle of the trip that this book has been. What we encounter in the middle is a passage largely unseen and unsignaled. Hardly anyone makes a stop at this point, unless there is a good reason to do so. It's a shame really, because everything begins here, well after beginning for the first time, with the first words of the opening pages. Similar to life itself, to existence and consciousness, a book begins in the middle, and it ends there, too: without an elementary preface, without a decisive conclusion. Actually, a book, a life, existence, and consciousness *begin to end* in the middle, feeding the beginning with the energy of the end. High noon, a day's midpoint, is when the sun starts to set. The time of "the shortest shadow," as Nietzsche expresses it, the zenith, is a premonition of the encroaching darkness.

The midpoint is thus a passage between the beginning and the end, or, more accurately, the end of the beginning and the beginning of the end. Passages are wonderfully ambiguous, both as far as their spatiotemporal boundaries and as far as the word's significations are concerned. They are channels and acts of transition, journeys and journeying, entrances or openings and long corridors, textual (extracts or excerpts) and contextual, pertaining to the right to travel and a way of escape. Passengers are passages in passages, journeying in a journey that journeys through them . . .

A smoothly running trip consists of all of the above: an unobstructed right to leave and enter places, a safe passage through them, making one's way through numerous corridors (the jet bridge or the gate sleeve between the airport and the aircraft, underground tunnels, travel corridors of approved routes in the age of pandemics, among many other things) and a vague awareness of available escape hatches. Meantime, passengers are bombarded with textual, musical, and visual passages that, darting from headsets and books, tablet and computer screens, public address systems, front seats, windows, or doors, compete for their attention chronically interrupted by announcements of departures and arrivals, new safety measures, and updates on the progress of the journey—the unfolding passage of the passage.

Passages are peculiar transfer stations between architectural structures and reading activities. Not as different from one another as we tend to imagine, works of architecture that preordain our movement through or around them and texts that dictate the rhythms of our readerly reception merge in the practice of interpretation. Guiding our orientation in space and in thinking (the latter is the subject of Kant's influential 1786 essay "What Does It Mean to Orient Oneself in Thinking?"), passages are the signposts for possible paths to be taken.

Every building has passages that may be inner or outer, covered on both sides as in a corridor or on one side only as in porticos or colonnades. In his fragmentary study of nineteenth-century Paris, Walter Benjamin, whom we have already encountered on the pages of this book, put an accent on the arcades that are, in his words, "the forerunners of our department stores."[1]

The arcades are passages: they are known in French as *passages couverts de Paris*, and the German title of Benjamin's project is *Passagenwerk*. The *passage* is a street, the buildings on both sides doubling as the walls of a corridor covered with an overhanging glass and metal ceiling. Also dubbed "the inner boulevards," the arcades facilitate the circulation of merchandise and buyers, the public space of the street snatched away from the outside world with its vulnerability to inclement weather, physically enclosed, and harnessed to the needs of commercial capital.

The Parisian *passages* are no longer thoroughfares, passages from one urban site to another, but places for loitering, promenading, passing time—in short, indulging in the favorite activities of the *flâneur*, all the while laying this time, energy, and life down on the altar of commerce. Aporetic, they are the passages of a nonpassage. In this, they presage the world of passengers that is our own. If, for Benjamin, arcade-strewn Paris was the capital of the nineteenth century, Nowhere is the capital of the twenty-first. Is our passengerhood in reading—our navigation of a colossal number of fragments, part-sentences, and clipped passages—equally adrift?

Stop no. 7: Reading, Riding

In the 1980s and early '90s, the years of my childhood in Moscow, Muscovites prided themselves on having the highest percentage of people in the world who read books while on public transport. When fellow passengers are reading, overcome by boredom or curiosity, we feel the temptation to join in. How often have you tried to glimpse the titles of the books they are immersed in, to follow the text itself or the news feed on their mobile devices, to peek at their messages and chats? Admit it or not, riding together is reading together, unintentionally gleaning passages from a wide array of sources that would not have been assembled were it not for meeting other readers-riders on a bus, a subway car, or a plane.

In and of itself, reading is a passenger exercise, for which it is not even necessary to leave the comfort of your own home. Our eyes travel on the page or on the screen, the gaze moving from letter to letter, word to word, sentence to sentence. Reading is experiencing in a nutshell. For a flash of a second, the reader snatches a portion of the text from relative obscurity only to let it slide back to dimness, retaining but a vague memory of what has been read. The same goes for experience in general: our mental regard zeroes in on a tiny bit from the flux of stimuli we are surrounded by, lets go of it, and keeps an unconscious or a semiconscious impression of what has been registered, linking it to what comes next. The read and the experienced pass through us, leaving behind the residue of memory, while we pass through the text and through the world, not without leaving our footprint, whether made of carbon or of other materials.

The mutuality of passing and passages we've just alighted upon means that, even as we are processing texts in all their mindboggling variety, we ourselves are processed by them and by the systems of transport that repeatedly swallow us up and spit us out in the uncanny metabolism of passenger society. Riding is not only reading (and vice versa) but also being read, translated into the self-recombining sequences of a code, pixelated information on video monitors, and quantified body data. While you are reading, the text looks back at you from the vegetal afterlife of the page or from the screen with its pale-blue glow; it returns an impersonal gaze over and above the stare of the face that is every surface, animate or inanimate. While you are riding in public transport, you are being read by ticket scanners and QR code readers that have either supplanted or supplemented human ticket controllers, not to mention body-temperature monitors, millimeter wave scanners, metal detectors, and the unblinking camera-eyes of surveillance networks. In a digitalized world, more than in any other period in history, you are a part of the text, fed into Big Data, inspected and deciphered by tireless algorithms.

Be this as it may, reading is an imperfect trap: it is a time machine and a space travel device that moves faster than the speed of light, proceeding at the speed of thought. A way of abstracting from the here-and-now, it is an ingenious contraption for visiting other countries, continents, and worlds, not to mention other epochs, past and future. You may do it without leaving the four walls of your room, or aboard a plane or train, on a boat or in a tram. Seated in the comfort of your sofa, your book or e-reader in hand, you are carried elsewhere and to another time; riding public transport, you are displaced in space and in your imagination, doubling (and, in a sense, overriding) your passenger experience. But, while it is peppered with escape routes, reading does not allow us to evade passengerhood; with its help, we can do no more than exchange one mode of being a passenger for another.

What happens as we read? I've sketched out above the dynamics of the reader's gaze, gliding on a page, registering letter- and word-sequences, interpreting them simultaneously with the act of registering, handing meaning over to the power of imagination, and, finally, committing it to a vague stratum of memory. But the functioning of our visual and cognitive radars is only half of the event of reading, which, on the obverse, entails our being scanned, our being read by a text in the state of captivation by that which incites our curiosity.

Organizing our thoughts and mental pictures from within, the foreign element of what is read is the locomotive that draws the train of understanding behind itself. We attach ourselves to it and let it haul us along ostensibly familiar tracks to hitherto unknown destinations. Now, this locomotive and the railcars it tugs along outstrip the simple model of attachment and detachment, the push and pull of repulsion and attraction. They also pass through us, but do so not without leaving a trace; to a certain extent, they become "us" by joining the web of images, metaphors, affects, and ideas, out of which our psychic life is woven. As passengers in the train of reading, we are also the tracks and the routes, along which the train travels, as well as this train itself.

The suggestive mix of passivity and activity in the figure of the passenger goes a long way toward explaining the author and reader positions in a text. Contrary to received opinion, the author is not the driving force (the captain or the conductor) of a book, a literary artifact that is as good as dead unless it finds a reader. The best authors do not have a commanding, authoritative voice, not to be conflated with that of a narrator; instead, they commend themselves to their own text, letting it unfurl in accord with its own inner logic. Exemplary readers, in their turn, are not herded along; they actively participate in the construction and the construal (i.e., the rewriting) of that which is read, even as they are carried along by the text at hand.

In keeping with this allocation of convergent positions to authors and readers, we may conclude that they are fellow passengers in the book they write and read. The literary proto-society we form is an asynchronous passenger society, where following, coming after, and going second are as much the activities of readers as they are of authors. We are all passengers of a vast text, which is unimaginably greater than the book you are now reading and, in reading it, rewriting—the text that includes not only whatever you've read today, this week, or this year, but also a spate of other texts your recent readings refer or allude to, refute, or rely upon. In other words, we are all passengers in the world of *intertextuality*, a term coined by the Bulgarian-French literary theorist and psychoanalyst Julia Kristeva to designate the subterranean connections between seemingly unrelated texts.

In addition to the mélange of activity and passivity, and besides the mix of authorly and readerly togetherness and loneliness, intertextuality stresses yet another paradoxical feature of literary passengerhood—haphazardness coupled with a rigid order. Suppose you pick a text at random. You skim through its lines without as much as noticing how it finds a slot next to other

We are all passengers of a vast text, which is unimaginably greater than the book you are now reading and, in reading it, rewriting.

writings that have left impressions in your memory, just like, by accident, other passengers are seated next to you in a subway car on aboard a plane. Yet, strictly speaking, every text resonates with any other text, as intertextuality has no limits, no clearly marked borders. If you look hard enough, you can spot the affinities between this book you are perusing now, a novel tucked away in your backpack or displayed on a bookshelf, a real estate brochure, a grocery list, the technical manual for your smartphone . . . The order of associations tightens still further if we take into consideration the class character and content of novels, real estate materials, and even grocery lists. Assuming that the passenger traveling in the seat next to you probably belongs to the same socioeconomic class as you, the intertextual universe, in which both of you rotate, plausibly encompasses similar constellations of texts.

Another aspect of passengerhood is excess, and it, too, haunts reading. The readerly excess is threefold: spatial overload, temporal overlay, and unconscious overflow. Both reading and riding revel in this excess, so much so that they manufacture the text and the world out of it. Especially on the road, we read all the time without intending to, nor making much of an effort: text messages that light up as soon as (or still before) we pick up our cellphones; car license plates; names of stores, stations, and stops; signs and billboards. We read these and many other things on the margins of attention, such that they are imprinted on our minds, largely bypassing conscious grasp. Akin to viruses, the readerly excess travels with us, in us, its sense emerging months or years later.[1]

As you read *Philosophy for Passengers*, you are welcome to extract random passages from the book, rearrange them to fit your mood, tailor them to your needs or to the time and place when and where you are. The text will survive and live on better, if it is not kept intact. But remember that, as a passenger, where you are now is where very soon you will no longer be. Which means that the task of reading and the work or the play of rearranging fragments we've read, whatever their source, is unending, resembling in this the incessant passages of passengers.

Stop no. 8: Security

Security is, no doubt, a keyword of our age, a universal hashtag of the twenty-first century. One of the most desirable intangible assets today, security is a scarce commodity. And the more it pops up in professional and lay discourse, the scarcer it is; oddly enough, in the age of security, insecurity is at its highest.

There is a sizable and growing disconnect between the formal and official uses of security, on the one hand, and the material reality of its privation, on the other. In international politics, global security studies (GSS) is a fast-growing field. In finance, marketable securities are cash substitutes that guarantee the liquidity of the companies that invest them on a short-term basis. In the havoc wreaked by global warming, climate security is a concept that emerged in reaction to the threats posed by rising sea levels, devastating droughts and floods, forest fires, catastrophic weather events, and crop failures. Compare these lucrative ventures and instruments with the lack of job security for the majority of workers around the world, the collapse of social security nets, the life-threatening insecurity of climate refugees and those hit hardest by pandemics. While a tiny fraction of the global population is profiting from the study and deployment of security (and insecurity), the rest are suffering the consequences.

The litmus test of security is the transport system. Both local and global, it is, rather than one part of the world among others, the quintessence of our volatile world, the condensation of the world's being and space-time. In the course of masterminding the Russian Revolution, Lenin knew that political control had to do, first and foremost, with success in seizing the infrastructure of communication and transport: the telegraph, the telephone, and railroad stations in and around Petrograd. The storming of the symbolic seat of monarchical power, the Winter Palace, came in a distant second by comparison to this objective. In the twentieth and twenty-first centuries, terrorist groups added to car bombings strikes on buses (for example, in Israel) and planes (as on 9/11 in the US). Targeting the means of passenger transport and the buildings they were diverted into, terrorist attacks aimed to impair nothing less than the modern world itself and its mobile foundations, something quietly accomplished on a larger scale by viral threats.

At this point, it is crucial to distinguish security from safety. Passenger manuals make it abundantly clear that safety is primarily related to (1) the means of transport as pieces of potentially malfunctioning technical equipment; (2) the elemental milieu (air, water, earth) through, over, or under which they move at high speeds; (3) extreme eventualities of undesirable situational interactions between (1), (2), and the bodies of passengers ("In the event of a water landing . . ."; "Stand away from the platform edge . . ."; "When onboard, hold on . . ."). Conversely, security spotlights threats posed by other human beings—say, the dangerous substances or weapons they might sneak aboard planes or trains. Safety is a technical issue; security is a social one. That is why we have safety certification, as opposed to security screening procedures.

In philosophical terms, the distinction between safety and security echoes the difference between *what* and *who* might be a source of danger, the difference we have touched upon with reference to cargo and passenger means of transport. Safety is ontico-technical, whereas security is ontologico-existential. In practical terms, the distinction betrays an absence of any objective criteria for security: no matter how thorough the screening procedures, there are countless ways to weaponize apparently harmless items. Of course, chance malfunctions in transport equipment may also happen, detailed safety checks notwithstanding. The landing gear of an aircraft may suddenly conk out, the brakes of a bus may stop working, a cruise ship may suffer an unforeseen engine failure, a train may derail due to buckling (or rail steel expansion in hot weather). But the perception of these and other similar causes is not on a par with security failures. Even if human *error* is behind a breach of safety protocols, it will not be judged as harshly as the *intent* to inflict damage by skirting security procedures.

It follows that security is intrinsically insufficient, making its unfillable lack a perfect excuse for continually tightening the measures associated with it. So, with a view to predicting and controlling the human factor in security breaches, the US Department of Homeland Security was, over the last decades, developing Project

Hostile Intent (PHI). This was an attempt to detect, interpret, and preemptively act upon the objective cues of planned malicious behavior, based on sensors, indicating pulse rates, body heat, sweating, and restlessness.[1] The technological infrastructure for the now (apparently) shelved project was to be implemented in major passenger hubs across the United States so as to "enhance border security and counter-terrorist operations." If PHI has indeed been abandoned rather than covered with an extra veil of secrecy, this is owing to its aspiration to do the impossible: to read purely outward signs as faithful expressions of the inner state, to capture existence with the aid of technology, to reduce the *who* of passenger security to a *what*.

The wisdom of language, too, hints at a gap between safety and security. Safety is a positive term, connoting wholeness, health and salvation, being or arriving literally "in one piece" (*salvus*, *solus*). For its part, security, in English and Romance languages (*sécurité*, *seguridad*, *segurança*, *sicurezza*, *securitate*), is the negation of care or concern (**se cura*), and the same etymology holds in Slavic languages (*bezpeka*, *bezpečnosti*, *bezpieczeństwo*).[2] This linguistic difference between two otherwise synonymous words is not trivial:

to the inflated hyperattention, bordering on paranoia, that was to be ingrained into passenger attitudes. Having since been adopted as the slogan of the Department of Homeland Security, the vague appeal to say something elliptically implores passengers to report potentially dangerous behaviors or items. But, given that just about anything you see in the tenebrous underworld of New York City may be tinged with worry, concern, and anxiety, you would have to communicate just about *everything* you see there to the authorities.

Second, the negation of care in the thick of "existential" apprehensions is utterly self-contradictory, because care is the stuff of which existence is made. Heidegger is adamant about this: "The being of human existence [*Dasein*] reveals itself as *care*. . . . No sooner has human existence [*Dasein*] expressed anything about itself to itself, than it has already interpreted itself as *care* (*cura*)."[3] Security goes to the heart of the matter—care/*cura*—which it proceeds to enucleate, denying, if we are to believe Heidegger, the cornerstone of human self-interpretation. This is not an abstract philosophical verdict, but evidence for the prioritization of sheer physical survival over and above a meaningful life. Like the transportation system that idolizes it, security becomes an end in itself, demanding the unconditional sacrifice of all else, including . . . security. A blatant example is the racial and religious profiling of passengers that "can lead to a climate of insecurity and fear" among the affected groups.[4]

The distinction between safety and security is not watertight, if only because our engagement with other people is intertwined with our interactions with things. When flight attendants urge you to place an oxygen mask on your face before assisting others in the event of an emergency, you participate in the inculcation of safety discourses with security measures. When you skim through lists of prohibited items, prominently displayed at airports, train stations, and similar transportation hubs, the opposite is going on: the safety or unsafety of objects tinges security deliberations. In either case, the system itself makes and expresses very specific assumptions about passengers. However technically necessary, the appeal to hold altruistic impulses in check reckons that these impulses are still active and encourages passengers to think about themselves first, to opt for an egoistic model of what it is to be human. The extensive and still growing lists of prohibited items confirm the conclusion that, if used with hostile intent, virtually anything may be a weapon: the potential of weaponization is infinite.

We thus return to the point of departure for our reflections on security, a slippery thing that is forever insufficient, and more so the tighter security measures get. Whether we are dealing with safety or security, it becomes clear that, like beauty, they are to be found exclusively in the eye of the beholder; they are feelings, beliefs, assurances (particularly, self-assurances).

After the COVID-19 pandemic first hit, a big international hotel chain rolled out its fresh campaign with the slogan "Feel safe!" Referring to enhanced disinfection procedures, this refrain was printed on hotel napkins, prominently displayed in elevators, and glued onto bottles of hand sanitizer generously strewn throughout the common areas. It occurred to me at the time that hotel management was not asking guests to *be* safe, only to *feel* safe. How could this be any different, if hotel guests and passengers are above all consumers, whose inclinations or inhibitions to keep on consuming their stays and travels are the only things that matter from the economic standpoint? And inclinations and inhibitions are sentiments, feelings operationalized, objectified, and measurable in consumer confidence indices. By the same token, the elaborate screening procedures and warnings at airports, train stations, and other transportation hubs scream out their true message to us: "*Feel* secure!"

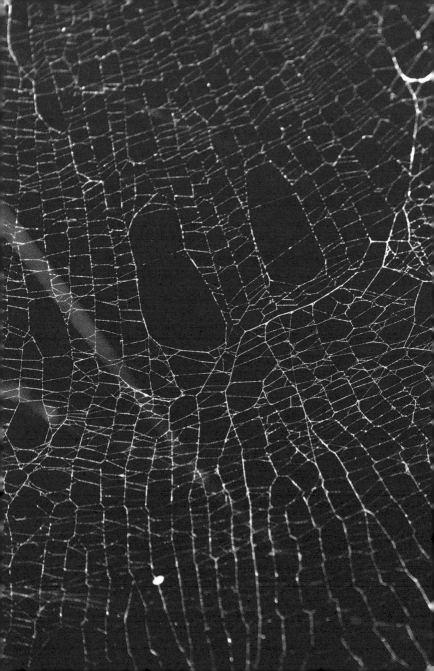

beasts and gods, of the infra- and suprahumans who live without the mediations of language, unites in itself many of the opportunities to quit the status of a passenger on the train of existence. Which amounts to saying that there is no way to shed one's passengerhood and stay alive, or, at least, to stay human.

The Yellow Arrow appears in the shape of a boundless chain of railcars, even to those who manage to train surf on it. "I could see neither the beginning nor the end of the train. Snaking several times in the field of vision, the line of railcars abutted both sides of the horizon. Nonetheless, the locomotive existed somewhere, and, besides a glut of intracar-metaphysical justifications, there were two clear proofs of its existence: the thick metallic cable situated about half a meter overhead and the occasionally audible, deriving God knows from where, quiet and prolonged humming."[2]

An all-encompassing train has important precedents in Russian literature and culture, some of them cited by Pelevin's characters. In the novel *The Foundation Pit*, written in the 1920s, Andrei Platonov pictures the nascent Soviet state as a bid to house all workers in the same mammoth building, for which they are to prepare, first, the foundation pit. The project does not move past the preparatory stage, the pit deepening and becoming a tomb for those who were to inhabit the structure. While, admittedly, Platonov imagines a total edifice, rather than a train, the effect of his literary exercise is comparable to that of Pelevin.

The train is also a potent symbol of the Russian Revolution, the civil war, and industrialization. From Boris Skorbin's 1918 song "Our Locomotive" ("Our locomotive is flying forward, / The next stop is the commune . . .") to the "agit-train" used by the Bolsheviks for propaganda purposes in the early 1920s, it came to represent the accelerated and inexorable progress of History toward a bright communist future. At the time of the collapse of the Soviet Union in the late 1980s and early 1990s, the same symbol evoked a collective catastrophe, from Boris Grebenshchikov's 1987 hit song "A Train on Fire," which Pelevin mentions in his short story, to Eldar Ryazanov's 1991 film *The Promised Heaven* with its emblematic ending where an old steam train bedecked with a red star and carrying a number of desperate passengers hits a dead end at full speed and, its wheels detaching from the rails, gracefully makes its way across the sky. Closer to Russia's passenger realities, "The Red Arrow" is the name of the overnight sleeper train that has circulated between Moscow and Leningrad (now St. Petersburg—yet another passenger of history) since 1931.

The cultural and historical background I have briefly reviewed just now neither explains away nor absorbs the shockwaves that ripple out from "The Yellow Arrow." The far-reaching existential implications of Pelevin's narrative are not limited to a national project, be it as universalist in its aspirations as the workers' revolution. An unstoppable train without a *why* and a *whither* is not merely an apt portrait of post-Soviet Russia but a sketch of the entire world. Along these lines, a newspaper Andrei skims through in the train's washroom lists regional and national onomatopoeic variations on "the most familiar and basic sound of our being," the rattle and resonance produced by train wheels as they roll along the rails: "In the US—'gingerale-gingerale'; in Baltic countries—'pa-duba-dam'; in Poland—'pan-pan'; in Bengal—'choog-choong'; in Tibet—'dzog-chen' . . ."[3] The cultural artifacts, surrounding the characters in the novella, include Boris Pasternak's 1943 collection *On Early Trains*, Akira Kurosawa's 1970 film *Dodes'ka-den*, and a *Guide to India's Railroads*, among other things.

What is to be done in the predicament of passengers who grow aware of their own passengerhood? Through Andrei and Khan, Pelevin proposes several solutions. Right after voicing his views on a "normal passenger," Khan concludes: "The most difficult thing in life is to travel by train without being its passenger."[5] It may seem as if, associating passengerhood with a purely passive attitude, he favors the active figure of the train conductor, but the proofs for the locomotive's (and, hence, the conductor's) existence are indirect, recalling, tongue-in-cheek, the metaphysical and theological proofs for the existence of God. The remaining option is traveling by train neither as a passenger nor as a conductor—an objective impossibility, which flips into a possibility only through a change of consciousness, that is, by attaining self-consciousness. One need not physically get off the train to cease being its passenger; merely knowing that one is a passenger is sufficient to quit this unwittingly accepted role. This is Pelevin's riff on the Delphic injunction *Know thyself!*, guiding Western thought from Socrates to Freud. The footnote that Pelevin adds to this long tradition is that, once you know who you are, you are no longer *that* (which you know yourself as), and your search must recommence.

Secretly, both Socrates and Freud were abreast of this condition: the former, eager to continue his quest even in the afterlife if there was such a thing; the latter, granting that psychoanalysis was an interminable endeavor.

The other solution, with which "The Yellow Arrow" draws to a close, is getting off the train. At first glance, within the structure of the story, this act presents itself as suicidal. Through the eyes of Andrei, we've seen passengers end up outside the train only after their death. But Pelevin is not a nihilist; what he asks for is a radical shift in perspective, this time around via a message Andrei receives from Khan, who is nowhere to be found on the train. The letter from his friend makes sense only after it is folded in two and read in this new way. Spelling out an inversion of the accepted order of things (e.g., "The past is the locomotive dragging the future behind itself . . ."), the missive claims to be a ticket not for boarding, but for getting off the train.[6] The crucial phrase in the letter, though, is its postscriptum: "Everything hinges on the fact that we constantly embark on a journey, which has already ended one second prior to our departure."[7]

To fathom that the journey we embark on "has already ended one second prior to our departure" is to get off the train without physically dying. The asynchrony between the events of our existence and our plans, fears and desires, representations and explanations, is the ticket for our detraining. "Who will you show this ticket to?" Khan's message inquires. Obviously, to yourself. The delay between consciousness and the world of which it is conscious, or between consciousness and self-consciousness, disorganizes time, passing the past for the present and the future (so that the "past is the locomotive . . ."). Such jumbling up of time is, far from a mistake, time itself.

The train of existence does not run on time, because time does not run on time. It is up to us to experience the disorganization of existence, which does not belong to the order of things, and to be jolted by it. Nothing palpable in the world, this experience makes all the difference. Pelevin plays here with the train-fate metaphor that has been prevalent in Russian literature since Tolstoy's *Anna Karenina*. He blends the metaphor with other raw materials for "The Yellow Arrow" and produces an effect that is the opposite of the customary one. The train of existence is fate incarnate, he insinuates, but we need not be fatalistic in our confrontations with it. In a moment of suspension, when the *already*

The train of existence does not run on time, because time does not run on time.

of arrival is the *not-yet* of departure, we can, following Khan, Andrei, and Pelevin himself, detrain without dying in the process. The past is no longer the locomotive then, uncoupled from the cars it has been dragging behind itself. Getting off the train is catching a ride on the intermittencies of existence, the asynchronies of passenger time, the disjointures of its joints.

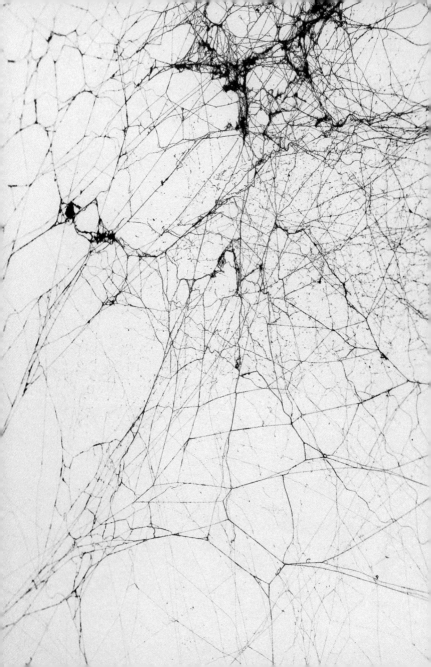

optimal separation from the sensed object, which, situated either too far or too close, becomes indiscernible. Other senses, such as touch, compel us to reduce our distance from the sensed surface to a minimum. But, across the board, all the senses of a living being are adjusted to its particular mode of life.

The sensory capacities proper to sessile life forms, including plants, mollusks, corals, and so on, boil down to carefully monitoring the changing environment around them. Although, upon receiving signs of danger, they cannot flee from the spot where they are, sessile creatures can activate defense strategies, modifying their physiological and, at times, morphological features. Growth is an exceptionally slow type of movement attuned to the subtle vibrations (for instance, via sensitive root tips) that allow it to be diverted from potential impasses and redirected to auspicious patches of soil or aboveground spaces. Distance senses give an advance warning of approaching danger, while touch enables the navigational orientation of growth.

The hypermodern condition of fast-moving transports and passengerhood exacerbates animal motility underpinning our sensory apparatus. As we've seen at Stop no. 3, what we are dealing with is not just a quantitative variation in the speeds, at which we make our way through the world. The senses struggle, often unsuccessfully, to catch up with the reality that is swishing by at the speed of 250 kilometers an hour (or more) on the other side of the glass. The ensuing maladjustment of the images, sounds, smells, tastes, and tactile impressions we are left with to the world jumbles the interfaces between reality and ourselves that the senses are. That is probably why passengers retreat into themselves, focusing on the ability to sense themselves sensing. Together with the senses, sense melts away, fading into the backdrop of suddenly appearing and disappearing patches of light, swiftly diverging and converging lines, roaring or hissing sounds, dimmed down smells, and places eluding touch.

The connections between the senses and sense (or meaning) are multiple. Experientially, the senses never receive raw data for subsequent processing and interpretation by our minds. Instead of hearing mere noise, we hear birds chirping or the squealing of breaks; rather than see wavelengths of light at 650 nm, we observe a reddish sunset. As soon as they receive impressions from the outside world, the senses conduct us to the sense of that which we perceive. They stimuli impoverishes our auditory, visual, and other sensory fields?

I want to stress in this regard two parallel phenomena: (1) *the senses of passengers*, or how passengers see, hear, smell, taste, and touch the world they pass through, and (2) *passenger senses*, or how our sensorium itself mutates to accommodate passenger societies and experiences. Let's go over the senses one by one in order to gauge the interplay of these phenomena in them.

Seeing

The *vision of passengers* is never direct. Mediated by glass and screens, it is markedly detached from the outside world, to which it nonetheless connects via these transparent separations. In intercity buses, in trains, and on planes, entertainment programs used to be played on TV sets suspended at the front and at regular intervals in the salon or the cabin, accessible to a group of passengers at the same time, while the audio feed was available through four or five channels prepared for individual headsets. Fragmenting the sensory object, the visual escape that a publicly displayed screen afforded was supplemented by a privately audible track. Next, screens were individually fitted for each seat on a plane, the visual experience of passengers further privatized. When the curtains or the shades are drawn, hiding from view the places passengers pass through, it seems that the only moving figures are those on screen. With the windows unobstructed, the impression one has is that passenger bodies and the contents of the conveyance they are riding in are perfectly still, even as the outside world is moving at a steady speed, accelerating or decelerating at times. This visual illusion proper to passengerhood reminds me of the pre-Copernican geocentric model of the universe: to passengers in motion, it appears that the world revolves around them, the places themselves rushing by until the right one comes into view.

Passenger vision is a mediated experience of seeing that interposes multiple screens, windows, transparent or semitransparent surfaces between the subject and the object of the gaze. As we glance at these material mediators, our gazes anonymously return to us: the surface, facing us, "looks" back and, every now and then, we see ourselves reflected, the reflection overlaid on the intended target of our regard. Since faint images of our faces hover over the places we pass or webpages we scroll through, there is a fair share of narcissism in this setup. But it also suddenly triggers self-awareness and disrupts our activities. Devices thought of as seamless technological channels interfere with the ocular workings they facilitate. More than that, passenger vision vacillates between the extremes it is ultimately incapable of integrating: on the one hand, it induces tunnel vision, blind to the context and spellbound by the destination; on the other, it promotes dispersion and distraction, a traveling gaze, tending in all directions at once. Peripheral vision leads a life of its own, separate from central vision. And fragmentation does not stop there. At the advanced stages of privatizing this passenger sense, we feel that we can draw the shades on the world at any moment, to stave off its light, to stop seeing the trees, cars, clouds, people, buildings, birds, lampposts, asphalt, and grass outside. But our screens are still aglow. It is easier to shut our eyes to physical than to digital reality.

Hearing

The auditory field, in which the *hearing of passengers* takes place, is filled with many noises: random fragments of conversations, laughter, crying babies, roaring engines, public announcements, squealing brakes, the rolling noise of wheels on rails . . . At first, it is difficult to discern anything but a terrible cacophony. Very quickly, though, we cease being conscious of the more monotonous among these sounds, as they peter out in an undifferentiated and no longer perceptible background. Others stand out because of their pitch, suddenness, jarring nature, and similar factors; in this way, portions of the auditory background break through to the foreground. To drown these jarring sounds out, passengers listen to music in their headphones, often at dangerously high-volume levels. Swapping one noisy background for another, the privatization of hearing proscribes listening. To listen to anything or anyone (in the first instance, to yourself), there needs to be silence, within which auditory reception germinates. Earplugs are a more radical passenger choice than headphones.

Passenger hearing is an evasion of silence. Wherever we are, whatever we do, we are uncomfortable with the perceived absence of sounds, the absence that can trigger feelings of loneliness, outward and inward emptiness, or anxiety. Ambient backgrounds of light and sound are created to tackle such unease, but, on their downside, they nourish a hearing without listening. Whenever we can, we live in our private soundscapes, the soundtracks we select for our existence, spasmodically pierced by the wailing of sirens, indicative of disasters nearby, and noises from neighboring units. Filtered through the digital sphere, the world arrives at our computer- or smartphone-doorsteps in sound-bites: mutilated, decontextualized. These fragments form a pervasive auditory background of our lives—the hallmark of passenger hearing, which individuates only excessive (loud, unanticipated, etc.) sounds. We are no longer able to listen to others nor, fundamentally, to hear ourselves.

Smelling

The *olfactory receptors of passengers* are assailed by exceptionally strong smells: fuel and burnt rubber, perfumes in duty-free areas and body odors of fellow passengers, food items brought from home and those served aboard, industrial-strength disinfectant sprays, used baby diapers, and aggressive air fresheners. Unlike vision and hearing, the olfactory sense cannot be dimmed: even wearing protective masks, we cannot shut our noses the way we close our eyes or plug our ears. The air, through which a medley of smells wafts, is a shared elemental milieu that is as inescapable as the chemicals that come to saturate it. Smells bring something of this shared nature with them, admitting, at the same time, individual and cultural differences in tolerance, perceptual thresholds, and meaningfulness of olfactory stimuli. They underscore passenger togetherness in aleatory social assemblages made, unmade, and remade in the means of transport. There is only one exception to the assault on passengers' sense of smell, and that is a pressurized aircraft cabin. Thanks to a combination of low air pressure and low humidity, the passengers' sense of smell is greatly diminished there. The high price we pay for mitigating olfactory unpleasantness is a temporary loss of this sensory faculty.

In *passenger smelling*, strong olfactory stimuli preponderate, having muscled fainter impressions out of meaningful perceptual space. They swell in a wave rippling through the air and hit us when we least expect it. We try to pass through places faster then, leaving the smells that give them their unique textures behind, and adding to them, for a brief moment, the odors of our perfumes, bodies, or car emissions. Olfactory neutrality implies habituation—to the point of not noticing a smell that always accompanies one—and the incapacity to discern delicate, faint scents owing to the high thresholds of sensitivity that strong stimuli set. Our noses are on a kind of rollercoaster ride: from a peak of effluvial assault, we drop to the valley of not smelling anything of note until the next peak. Just as we do not linger in the places we zip by, so we do not tarry with smells that give places their depth, emotional tonality and atmospheric feel. A biochemical medley of a small number of overpowering aromas, passenger smelling is a sensory signature of our relation to places, to the milieu, in which we move and which moves in and through us.

Tasting

The *tastes of passengers* obey the double imperative of the simplification and amplification of stimuli valid for all sensory domains. Apart from the niche market

Our noses are on a kind of rollercoaster ride: from a peak of effluvial assault, we drop to the valley of not smelling anything of note until the next peak.

of "gourmet" meals at train stations, airports, and first-class cabins, the food served on the go is, precisely, fast food. With the preparation and consumption of meals sped up, as the term "fast food" indicates, the gustatory function must be subject to rapid and powerful stimulation. There is no time to waste on a gradual discovery of flavors and aftertastes. This is where exceptionally salty or sweet food items fit in, introduced to mask the underlying blandness of a snack, a sandwich, or a side order. At high altitudes, moreover, the biochemistry of taste buds changes in tandem with the sense of smell (flavor is, essentially, a combination of both senses): our perception of saltiness and sweetness is blunted in a pressurized cabin 10,000 meters above ground.

Passenger tastes embrace superficial newness, speed, and the overstimulation of taste receptors. "New" flavors, derived from chemical additives, may momentarily appeal to consumers until the next gustatory novelty item pops up on the market. Frozen meals, takeout packages, and, of course, fast food are readily available for a life on the go, the life of passengerhood. The contents of these meals appeal in a disproportionate manner to basic tastes—notably, salty and sweet, to the exclusion of sour and bitter—because they are

the veil of anonymity and in conditions severely restricting the freedom of bodily movement, the act revels in deindividuated and deindividuating touch.

Passenger touching is the gliding of the hand and of the fingers over a screen, a keyboard, and a limited number of other surfaces making up much of our tactile environment. We touch the world in passing, our fingers already bolting elsewhere, having barely gotten closer to the nearby surfaces. And we are out of touch with the world that we fleetingly touch, restricting the range of our tactile surroundings to manufactured objects. Petting a dog or a cat is a poor substitute for nonsynthetic textures that are for the most part lacking within the reach of our hands. When was the last time you touched tree bark, sand, or moist earth? Food items, too, arrive in our kitchens already highly processed, wrapped in plastic or resting on Styrofoam. With some cultural variations (themselves decimated, temporarily or not, by the COVID-19 pandemic), being in touch, verbally communicating to other people, rarely entails physically touching them. More and more, we come to others and leave them empty-handed: our hands grasp air, our fingertips caressing, at most, smooth and cold "touchscreens." What does this tactile impoverishment do to our brains (and especially to a developing child's brain), given the extensive stimulation of the somatosensory cortex by signals that originate in touch receptors? In passenger touching, the most grounded, the most materially involved among the senses is rarefied, nearly lapsing into abstraction. The sentient body turns into a deficient replica of a disembodied mind, sweeping through a touchless world.

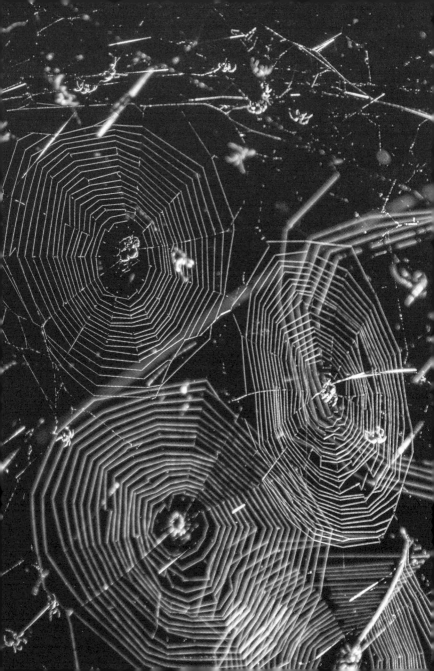

Stop no. 10: Destination, Destiny

Once upon a time, the goddesses of destiny were feared and revered. The Greek Moirai and the Roman Parcae had tremendous power over mortals, guiding the journey of life from birth to death. Human beings were destined to participate in a unique constellation of events and fated to go to their demise in a certain manner, preordained from the very beginning or, maybe, still before the beginning, before birth. Pointless were attempts to fight one's fate. Irrespective of a person's will, desire, and resolve to dodge cosmic or divine pincers, the iron law of fate was that the greater the resistance you offered to what awaited you, the tighter the grip in which you found yourself. Resistance merely fast-forwarded the film of your life to its not so happy end. The ancient story of Oedipus, who tried unsuccessfully to counter the prophecy that he would kill his father and marry his mother, amply proves this point.

The terms *destiny* and *fate* present themselves to us as linguistic twins. But they are as different from one another as safety and security. Destiny is tailormade for each; fate is the same for all. Destiny is the path; fate is the destination. Destiny pushes us from behind, like wind in a ship's sails; fate pulls us from ahead, like a locomotive. This push-and-pull recedes from modern consciousness, suspicious of anything that deprives individuals of their formal freedom and self-making abilities. For all intents and purposes, it remains only in certain occult practices: tarot card readings, crystal-gazing, palmistry, or astrology.

In daily life, a vague and distorted memory of destiny is preserved in our destinations, to which we travel by various means of transport. In Portuguese, for example, the word *destino* encompasses both destiny and destination. That you travel to your *destino* together with throngs of other passengers is a sign of the times, the times of massifying life and death. Destinations are among the few things through which the meaning of destiny still shines, if only vaguely. This light is nonetheless refracted through the concept of fate, which destiny/destination came to supplant: the route of a life or of the activities that fill it are transferred onto the terminal point of that route. Which is to say that there is no terminal point anymore, nothing that pulls one from ahead, no end and no ends in sight.

The last stop of a route does not matter at all, unless it coincides with the destination *you* are traveling toward. This point is both last and not last: it is the objective terminus for the means of transport that will travel back along the same tracks, or fly, drive, or sail elsewhere from there, and it is a subjective arbitrary marker, in case you need to make a transfer after or leave at any prior stop along the route. In a similar fashion, fate and destiny lose their finality. There are plenty of itineraries you can construct to reach the same destination (if not by train, then by plane; if not with a direct flight, then by taking several connecting ones, you will get there) and there are as many reasons for changing your destination, too. Nothing seems predetermined, predestined or fated to happen. Everything is within your power, within the scope of means without ends that is technology as the framework for being as such.

Is the last stop of your own itinerary today any different from that of the air, land, or sea routes along which you are traveling as a passenger? It is not that you are uninterested in the actual destination of your journey, even though you may fall asleep during the trip or get so deeply immersed in your thoughts or a book you are reading that you miss your stop—something I've experienced myself on more than one occasion. What I mean is that, in the dispersion of our existence, unfolding along multiple and rarely synchronized timescales and schedules, arrivals are, simultaneously, nonarrivals. Each second is filled with an overwhelming array of events and processes claiming our passenger senses and minds, time- and space-consciousness, attention, memory, and anticipation. We always arrive at our destinations prematurely, too late, or both, the body or the mind lagging behind or running ahead, the next project displacing the current one from the sphere of concern. You are always traveling elsewhere than the destination, at which you have just arrived.

Portuguese poet Fernando Pessoa ruminates about the condition of nonarrival in passenger arrival as he (or his semi-heteronym, Bernardo Soares) recalls daydreaming during a train ride between the resort town of Cascais and Lisbon: "I daydream between Cascais and Lisbon. . . . I took anticipated pleasure in the trip, anticipated pleasure is frustrated; frustration mounts in an effort to mentally nail down missed opportunities; the efforts to catch up with the past rob him of sensations in the present . . . until, having completed a return trip, the train arrives at its destination, the terminal station of Cais do Sodré in Lisbon.

The arrival at the station, the *destino* of Pessoa's voyage, does not bring closure to the disappointments and nonaccomplishments that have accrued during the train ride. Hence, his famous non sequitur line—and a well-constructed sequence of ideas is also said to be a *train of thought*—"I have arrived at Lisbon, but not at a conclusion," holding one of the keys to passengerhood. To be a passenger is to be suspended in the rift between *destino* and *destino*, between destiny and destination, between each destination and itself, between one destination and another already showing up on the horizon or inside the territory of the first. Nonaccomplishment, noncoincidence—right at the destination that is within reach and that has already slipped away from us.

Our lives and desires are not predestined to unfurl along a single path seeing that, from the get-go, they are scattered, tending in several, sometimes mutually exclusive directions. What is the destiny of something (or someone) as unwieldy as that? We are driven on by nonaccomplishment, by our noncoincidence with ourselves, by the nonarrival in each arrival. The calm of rest, in which the constant *Not enough!* of desire might be quelled, scares us to death; in fact, it presents itself to us as nothing but death, itself euphemistically equated to a passage, a passing away, as we have observed. When we are no longer or not yet passengers, we get edgy, feeling that our lives are stagnating. And, conversely, we live inasmuch as we lose ourselves, in keeping with Pessoa's turn of phrase. The more thoroughly we lose ourselves in ruminations or entertainment, in the passages within passages of life, the more alive we feel. Satisfaction is suspect. We hear in *Enough!* an admission of defeat, as in *I've had enough! I've reached the end of the road!*

Destinations, then, are fresh points of departure, keeping alive the hope that our destiny has not led us here, to the place where we are or toward which we are heading at the moment, as to our very last stop. The essentially American faith in social mobility belongs together with this hope, in contrast to the British, all-too-British injunction, intended to put one back in one's place, not to get ideas "above one's station." Our optimism conceals the awareness (which irrupts in moments of lucid sadness or tranquil acceptance, such as those strewn across the biblical book of Ecclesiastes) that this too shall pass, that everything will pass and I will pass with everything. Ongoing passengerhood, our moving past every conceivable destination, is mobilized to repel these breakthrough insights. We console ourselves with the thought that, so long as we are passengers who are undetained at any single stop, we will not pass (away) amidst the passing of everything, nor will the passages themselves, in which we keep circulating, disappear. In the turbulence of our world, we marshal passing against passing, passengerhood against the fugaciousness of all that is, the absence of a final destination against the destinies of ecological, cultural, and social devastation.

We might never arrive at our destinations, rejoicing in or bemoaning our nonarrival. Still, destinations will modulate the vectors of our movement, in the same manner that certain types of behavior (say, smoking or doing physical exercise) combined with environmental factors (air pollution, pesticides in foodstuffs) will raise or lower the probabilities of contracting a serious disease in the future. What nonarrival does mean is that destinations will not welcome us, will not receive us in themselves, even if someone is waiting for us somewhere—the beloved, a friend, a colleague, a child, a dog, a houseplant. Together with all other places, destinations are marked by the same nonacceptance as our attitude to destiny. Is there anything we can do to mend this state of things, that is, to suffuse destinations with hospitality toward the passengers heading there?

Let's listen to Nietzsche's advice. "'Chance' is what the weak call it. But I say to you: what could befall me that my gravity would not compel and draw to itself? Look, will you, how I first stew each coincidence in my juices: and when it is done, it means, for me, 'my will and destiny.' Whatever it is about my chance that seems foreign to my body and will, how could I offer hospitality to that! Look, will you, only friends approach friends."[2]

To begin with, Nietzsche implores us, welcome your destiny as part of who you are—offer hospitality to what seems foreign to your body and will. Allowing such apparently alien elements as coincidences to stew in our own juices makes them doubly ours, after they have been drawn to us, as though by the force of gravity, expressed more broadly in the law that like attracts like, "only friends approach friends." Once we accept that what befalls us apparently at random is part of who we are, once we welcome our destinies, our destinations, too, will accept us in themselves, opening up a world where abiding and dwelling might be possible.

Disembarking

Everything in life comes to an end, and so do books, including this one. Are you ready to disembark, then? But not so fast! Infinitely finite, existence presses on. You might not be able to disembark, yet you must disembark. Samuel Beckett voiced this paradox well in *The Unnamable*: ". . . impossible to stop, impossible to go on, but I must go on, I'll go on, without anyone, without anything but me, but my voice, that is to say I'll stop, I'll end, it's the end already . . ."[1]

When you detrain, deplane, or leave a ship, who disembarks? What disembarks? While your body is still aboard, your mind could be roaming very far away from the means of transport where you are seated, or, vice versa, while your feet are still on the ground, your thoughts could be high up in the clouds or carried by ocean waves. When does a trip end? When you step off a vessel, an aircraft, a bus, or a train? When does reading stop? When you close a book and put it on a shelf? Is there such a clear cutoff point? Doesn't the process keep moving, unfolding, as though by inertia, even after the passenger experience of riding or reading has been terminated, has reached its terminal point or terminus? Doesn't any experience whatsoever, for which passengerhood stands nowadays, continue after it has actually finished?

One weird feature of human understanding is that we start comprehending things when we no longer experience them directly. The voyage of understanding begins after a journey of perception and cognition in the world has ended: this insight is shared by Hegel and contemporary psychoanalysts, for instance, the Canadian psychologist and education specialist Deborah Britzman.[2] In this sense, disembarking is both the end and a new beginning, which may rerun on another screen (of memory, analysis, and *re*cognition) the path you have just traversed. The question is: which experience will you turn your attention to after flipping the last page? That of having read the book *Philosophy for Passengers*? Of having been a passenger in a public

The voyage of understanding begins after a journey of perception and cognition in the world has ended.

means of transport? Of experiencing the world and yourself? All of the above, fused into the general haze of stimulation, undergoing, acting, and desiring that is your life?

A Note on Images

Through floating sculptures, interactive installations, and artistic processes that center on collaboration, artist Tomás Saraceno proposes a conversation between human and nonhuman lifeforms that have been disregarded in the Capitalocene era, such as the air, spiders and their webs, and compromised communities. Argentine born and Berlin based, Saraceno has worked with local communities, scientific researchers and institutions around the world, including the communities of Somie, Cameroon; Salinas Grandes, Argentina; Massachusetts Institute of Technology; Max Planck Institute; and Nanyang Technological University, among others. In a call for environmental justice, Saraceno's artistic collaborations renew relationships with the terrestrial, atmospheric, and cosmic realms, particularly as part of his community projects, *Aerocene* and *Arachnophilia.*

Aerocene is an era free from borders and fossil fuels, a common imaginary for an ethical re-alliance with the environment, the planet and the cosmic/web of life beyond Anthropocentrism. Initiated by artist Tomás Saraceno and developed through a community-based approach, *Aerocene* has collectively launched 110 tethered flights, 15 free flights, and 8 human flights. One artwork series included in this book reveals shots from the *Aerocene* project *Fly with Aerocene Pacha.* On January 25, 2020, the aerosolar sculpture *Aerocene Pacha* flew with the message "Water and Life are Worth More than Lithium" written with the communities of Salinas Grandes, Jujuy, Argentina. Floating completely free from fossil fuels, batteries, lithium, solar panels, helium, and hydrogen, 32 world records, recognized by the Fédération Aéronautique Internationale (FAI), were set by *Aerocene* pilot Leticia Noemi Marqués. This marks the most sustainable flight in human history, and one of the most important experiments in the history of aviation.

Saraceno also founded the transdisciplinary *Arachnophilia* research project, and worked collaboratively with spider/webs (and the research community they attract) for over twelve years. His fascination with spider/webs is grounded in a persistent curiosity about how we might construct more sustainable and ecologically just futures, through radical practices of attunement with arachnid kin. Saraceno's interspecies research endeavors and forays into the vibratory Umwelten of spider/webs continue to probe the possibilities for thinking, doing, and becoming-otherwise. Formed of complex interwoven networks suspended in air, the other artwork series presents the unique architectures of *Hybrid Spider/Webs*, which originate from interspecific encounters between unrelated solitary, social, and semisocial spider species. From these encounters emerges a space where multitudes observe themselves in the very act of becoming a community: a spatial condition of physical immersion in an environment where stories of coexistence between humans and other species materialize.

Let's travel together toward an atmosphere of ecological sensitivity and symbiotic mutualism.

Tomás Saraceno would like to give special thanks to Michael Marder for the opportunity to contribute to *Philosophy for Passengers*.

Thanks also to Studio Tomás Saraceno, especially Lars Behrendt, Sarah Kisner, Manuela Mazure, Claudia Meléndez, Jillian Meyer, Dario Lagana, Lucas Mateluna, and Gustavo Alonso Serafin.

To the *Aerocene* and Museo Aero Solar communities, especially project participants of *Fly with Aerocene Pacha* including the 33 communities of Salinas Grandes represented by Res Pozos, Tres Morros, Pozo Colorado & San Miguel del Colorado, as well as *Aerocene* pilot Leticia Marqués, curator DaeHung Lee, and project supporters Veronica Fiorito and Maristella Svampa. The sculpture *Aerocene D-OAEC* was made possible by the support of Christian Just Linde. Special thanks to Eric and Caroline Freymond for their generous, long-term support of *Aerocene*.

To the *Arachnophili*a research community, especially Ally Bisshop and Roland Muehlethaler with Nephila inaurata, Nephila edulis, Nephila senegalensis, Cyrtophora citricola, Holocnems pluchei, Agelena labyrinthica, Eratigena, (Tegenaria) atrica, Tegenaria domestica, Araneus diadematus, Larinioides sclopetarius,

A Note on Images

Badumna longinqua, as well as *Arachnophilia* community members Markus Buehler, Evan Ziporyn, and Leila Kinney of MIT; Ian Couzin and Alex Jordan of Max Planck Institut; Peter Jäger of Senckenberg Research Institute & Natural History Museum; Jonas Wolff of Macquarie University; and Hannelore Hoch and Andreas Wessel of Berlin Museum für Naturkunde, among many others.

To Andersen's, Copenhagen; Ruth Benzacar, Buenos Aires; neugerriemschneider, Berlin; Pinksummer Contemporary Art, Genoa; and Tanya Bonakdar, New York/Los Angeles.

And to all the friends and family dreaming together toward renewed relationships with the terrestrial, atmospheric, and cosmic realms.

List of Images

"Ticketing": Tomás Saraceno, *Solitary, semi social mapping of Q0906+6930 by one Nephila clavipes—two weeks, a pair of Cyrtophora citricola—one week*, 2015. Courtesy the artist. © Tomás Saraceno.

"Preboarding": Tomás Saraceno, *Detail of a Latrodectus mactans web*, 2017. Courtesy the artist. Special thanks to the Arachnophilia Community. © Tomás Saraceno.

"The Boarding Process (A): The Basics": Tomás Saraceno, *Galaxies Forming along Filaments, Like Droplets along the Strands of a Spider Web*, 2018. Courtesy the artist. © Tomás Saraceno.

"The Boarding Process (B): The Passenger Society": Tomás Saraceno, *Galaxies Forming along Filaments, Like Droplets along the Strands of a Spider Web*, 2018. Courtesy the artist. © Tomás Saraceno.

"Stop no. 1: Mood": *Fly with Aerocene Pacha*, a project by Tomás Saraceno for an Aerocene era. On the January 25, 2020, thirty-two world records, ratified by FAI, were set by Aerocene with Leticia Noemi Marques, flying with the message "Water and Life are Worth More than Lithium" written by the communities of Salinas Grandes, Jujuy, Argentina. This marks the most sustainable flight in human history. *Fly with Aerocene Pacha* was produced by the Aerocene Foundation and Studio Tomás Saraceno. Supported by Connect, BTS, curated by DaeHyung Lee. First exhibited at CCK, curated by Veronica Fiorito. © Tomás Saraceno.

"Stop no. 2: Time": Tomás Saraceno, *Aerocene flight above the glaciers of Chamonix*, 2019. Courtesy the artist. © Tomás Saraceno.

"Detour no. 1: ¡No Pasarán!": *Fly with Aerocene Pacha*, a project by Tomás Saraceno for an Aerocene era. © Tomás Saraceno.

"Stop no. 3: Place": Tomás Saraceno, *Aerocene flight above the glaciers of Chamonix*, 2019. Courtesy the artist. © Tomás Saraceno.

"Stop no. 4: Existence": *Fly with Aerocene Pacha*, a project by Tomás Saraceno for an Aerocene era. © Tomás Saraceno.

"Detour no. 2: Passengers, Hollywood Style": Tomás Saraceno, detail view of *Weaving the Cosmos*. Exhibited in *Weaving the Cosmos*, Planetario Ulrico Hoepli, Milan, 2018. Courtesy the artist. © Tomás Saraceno.

"Stop no. 5: Transport": Tomás Saraceno, detail view of *Webs of At-tent(s)ion*. Exhibited in *On Air, Carte Blanche à Tomás Saraceno*. Palais de Tokyo, Paris, 2018. Courtesy of the artist. © Tomás Saraceno.

"Stop no. 6: Metaphor": Tomás Saraceno, *Solitary semi-social mapping of SXDF-NB1006–2 by one Nephila clavipes—one week, one Tegenaria domestica—eight weeks and a pair of Cyrtophora citricola—one week*, 2015. Courtesy the artist. © Tomás Saraceno.

"Connection/Transfer: Passages": *Fly with Aerocene Pacha*, a project by Tomás Saraceno for an Aerocene era. © Tomás Saraceno.

"Stop no. 7: Reading, Riding": Tomás Saraceno, *Hybrid solitary semi-social SAO 80113 built by: a solo Nephila senegalensis—two weeks, a sextet of Cyrtophora citricola—one week, rotated 90°*, 2020. Courtesy the artist. © Tomás Saraceno.

"Stop no. 8: Security": Tomás Saraceno, detail view of *Webs of At-tent(s)ion*. Exhibited in *On Air, Carte*

Blanche à Tomás Saraceno. Palais de Tokyo, Paris, 2018. Courtesy of the artist. © Tomás Saraceno.

"Detour no. 3: 'The Yellow Arrow'": Tomás Saraceno, *Gravitational solitary Choreography SAO 19302 built by: a duet of Nephila senegalensis—six weeks*, 2021. Courtesy the artist. © Tomás Saraceno.

"Stop no. 9: Senses": Tomás Saraceno. *Solitary, semi-social mapping of The Southern Pinwheel with neighbouring galaxies, by one Nephila clavipes—three weeks and twelve Cyrtophora citricola spiderlings—four weeks*, 2015. Courtesy the artist. © Tomás Saraceno.

"Stop no. 10: Destination, Destiny": Tomás Saraceno, detail view of *Quasi-social musical instrument IC 342 built by: 7000 Parawixia bistriata—six months*. Exhibited in *How to Entangle the Universe into a Spider Web?* Museo de Arte Moderno de Buenos Aires, 2017. Courtesy the artist. © Tomás Saraceno.

"Disembarking": *Fly with Aerocene Pacha*, a project by Tomás Saraceno for an Aerocene era. © Tomás Saraceno.

Notes

Ticketing

1. See, for instance, Alain de Botton, *The Art of Travel* (New York: Vintage, 2004); Daniel Klein, *Travels with Epicurus: A Journey to a Greek Island in Search of a Fulfilled Life* (London: Penguin, 2012); Emily Thomas, *The Meaning of Travel: Philosophers Abroad* (Oxford: Oxford University Press, 2020).
2. Martin Heidegger, *Nietzsche*, volume 2: *The Eternal Recurrence of the Same*, trans. David Farrell Krell (New York: Harper & Row, 1984), 200.
3. Metaphysics may be thought of as the fixed and ideal field of things that do not pass, the field of eternal things prone neither to metamorphosis nor to metabolism.
4. See Michael Marder, *Dust* (New York: Bloomsbury, 2016).

The Boarding Process (A)

1. "*Passager, -ère*," in Émile Littré, *Dictionnaire de la langue française* (Paris: Hachette, 1900), 820.

The Boarding Process (B)

1. Francesca Friday, "More Americans Are Single Than Ever Before—And They're Healthier, Too," *Observer*, January 16, 2018, https://

observer.com/2018/01/more-americans-are-single-than-ever-be
fore-and-theyre-healthier-too.

2. Hannah Arendt, *The Origins of Totalitarianism* (New York: Harcourt Brace, 1976), 478.

3. Arendt, *Origins of Totalitarianism*, 478.

4. Robert Bird and Frank Newport, "What Determines How American Perceive Their Social Class?" *Gallup Polling Matters*, February 27, 2017, https://news.gallup.com/opinion/polling-matters/204497 /determines-americans-perceive-social-class.aspx.

5. Another fantasy contained in the slogans like "America First!," "Brazil First!," "Hungary First!" is that the forces espousing them are against globalism and cosmopolitanism. In fact, the first implies the second, which means that the slogan and the idea it expresses are invested in the creation of *world society*, however asymmetrical the positions of its participants vis-à-vis each other.

Stop no. 1

1. For nonhuman people, see Timothy Morton, *Humankind: Solidarity with Non-Human People* (London: Verso, 2019).

2. Martin Heidegger, *Being and Time*, trans. John Macquarrie and Edward Robinson (New York: Harper & Row, 1962), 173, translation modified.

3. Iain McIntosh, "Travel Phobias," *Journal of Travel Medicine* 2 (1995): 99–100.

4. Jacques Derrida and Catherine Malabou, *Counterpath: Traveling with Jacques Derrida*, trans. David Wills (Stanford: Stanford University Press, 2004), 5.

5. Walter Benjamin, *Illuminations: Essays and Reflections*, trans. Harry Zohn (New York: Schocken Books, 2007), 239.

6. Friedrich Nietzsche, *Unpublished Fragments (Spring 1885–Spring 1886)*, trans. Adrian Del Caro, *The Complete Works of Friedrich Nietzsche*, vol. 16 (Stanford: Stanford University Press, 2019), 323.

Stop no. 2

1. In line with Hegel's philosophy, a thing at its zenith already displays clear signs of decline: *Phenomenology* plays with the difference between the phenomenological perspective at various stages (or stations) of spirit and its absolute destination. In the interplay between them, the epic impulse is, at the same time, preserved and cancelled out, or, in a word, sublated (*aufgehoben*).

2. Jean Robert, *Les tramways parisiens* (Paris: G. Fuseau, 1959), 18.

Detour no. 1

1. Dolores Ibárruri Gómez, *They Shall Not Pass: The Autobiography of La Pasionaria* (New York: International Publishers, 1966).

2. Acisclo Muñiz Vigo, *El Generalísimo Franco en la escuela española: Bosquejo biográfico, efemérides, lecturas, miscelánea* (Oviedo: Editorial F.E.T, 1939), 67.

3. J. G. Fichte, *Foundations of Natural Right*, trans. Michael Baur (Cambridge: Cambridge University Press, 2000), 257.

Stop no. 3

1. G. W. F. Hegel, *Philosophy of Nature: Encyclopedia of the Philosophical Sciences, Part II*, trans. A. V. Miller (Oxford: Oxford University Press, 2004), 29.

2. G. W. F. Hegel, *Hegel's Phenomenology of Spirit*, trans. A. V. Miller (Oxford: Oxford University Press, 1977), 61.

3. Michael Marder, *Grafts: Writings on Plants* (Minneapolis: University of Minnesota Press, 2016), 158.

Stop no. 4

1. René Descartes, *Meditations on First Philosophy*, trans. Michael Moriarty (Oxford: Oxford University Press, 2008), 13–14.

Stop no. 5

1. The same can be said about "cruises to nowhere," pioneered in Singapore in the same year.

Stop no. 6

1. Ivor Armstrong Richards, *The Philosophy of Rhetoric* (Oxford: Oxford University Press, 1965), 94.
2. Steven C. Hayes, Kirk D. Strosahl, Kelly G. Wilson, *Acceptance and Commitment Therapy, Second Edition: The Process and Practice of Mindful Change*, 2nd ed. (New York: Guilford Press, 2012), 251.
3. Donald J. Orth, David D. Schmitt, and Corbin D. Hilling, "Hyperbole, Simile, Metaphor, and Invasivore: Messaging About Non-Native Blue Catfish Expansion," *Fisheries Magazine*, July 17, 2020, https://doi.org/10.1002/fsh.10502.

Connection/Transfer

1. Walter Benjamin, *The Arcades Project*, trans. Howard Eiland and Kevin McLaughlin (Cambridge, MA: Belknap Press, 1999), 15.

Stop no. 7

1. Similarly, marketing specialists bet on the sudden resurfacing of the contents of commercials from the depths of the unconscious

during shopping and in other moments when a person feels the otherwise inexplicable urge to purchase a previously advertised item or experience.

Stop no. 8

1. "Project Hostile Intent," *AIR: American Institutes for Research*, https://www.air.org/project/project-hostile-intent.
2. In Russian, the word for security is *bezopasnost'*, or, literally, "dangerlessness." The Russian *bespechnost'*, which technically reproduces words for security in other Slavic languages (notably, Polish, Ukrainian, and Czech), actually means "carelessness."
3. Heidegger, *Being and Time*, 227.
4. Lee Ferran, "Delicate Balance: Airline Security vs. Personal Privacy," *ABC News*, December 27, 2009, https://abcnews.go.com/GMA/airline-security-threat-privacy-airport-body-scanning/story?id=9430705.

Detour no. 3

1. Viktor Pelevin, *Zheltaya Strela* [The Yellow Arrow] (Moscow: FTM, 2007), 20. This and all subsequent translations of Pelevin's text are mine.
2. Pelevin, *Zheltaya Strela*, 26.
3. Pelevin, *Zheltaya Strela*, 19.
4. Pelevin, *Zheltaya Strela*, 11.
5. Pelevin, *Zheltaya Strela*, 11.
6. Pelevin, *Zheltaya Strela*, 35.
7. Pelevin, *Zheltaya Strela*, 35.

Stop no. 10

1. Fernando Pessoa, *The Book of Disquiet*, trans. Richard Zenith (New York: Penguin, 2003), 23.
2. Friedrich Nietzsche, *Unpublished Fragments from the Period of Thus Spoke Zarathustra (Summer 1882–Winter 1883/84)*, trans. Paul S. Loeb and David F. Tinsley, *The Complete Works of Friedrich Nietzsche*, vol. 14 (Stanford: Stanford University Press, 2019), 548.

Disembarking

1. Samuel Beckett, *Three Novels: Molloy, Malone Dies, The Unnamable* (New York: Grove Press, 2009), 388.
2. Refer to Deborah Britzman, *After-Education: Anna Freud, Melanie Klein, and Psychoanalytic Histories of Learning* (Albany, NY: SUNY Press, 2003).